CONTENTS

Introduction

How will this book help me?

How should I use this book?

What is in the Modern Studies course?

What is the Modern Studies exam like?

How do I use statistical sources?

Will this book give me the content I need for the exam?

What is in this book?

HOW WILL THIS BOOK HELP ME?

This book is designed to teach and improve the skills necessary to do well in Modern Studies. You may be taking Intermediate Modern Studies as an S3/S4 course at school or in S5/6 following an earlier Standard Grade course. You may be studying Modern Studies at college. At the end of your course, you may sit the examination at Intermediate 1 level or at Intermediate 2. For some of you, Modern Studies may be a fairly new subject; others of you will have studied the subject before and practised many of the necessary skills. Whatever your situation, this book will help you to achieve success and the best possible grade in your exam.

HOW SHOULD I USE THIS BOOK?

This is not the sort of book you will get the most out of by reading it straight through from beginning to end. You should use this book as and when you need it. There are sections on how to answer all the different types of questions you will come across – in unit assessments, in school exams and, most importantly of all, in your final SQA examination. During your course, you should look at different sections of this book when you are attempting particular types of questions in order to develop your skills. It may be useful to look at particular sections several times until you are confident with your own skills.

The book covers skills at Intermediate 1 and Intermediate 2 levels. These levels cover the same study themes and topics, so you will recognise the topics in the questions whatever level you are studying. If you are sitting the examination at Intermediate 1 level, you may find many of the Intermediate 2 questions quite difficult. Even if you intend to sit Intermediate 2 in the final exam, at the start of the course you may also find some of the Intermediate 2 questions quite difficult. However, you can develop your skills by practising Intermediate 1 questions to begin with. This will help you build your skills to Intermediate 2 level.

WHAT IS IN THE MODERN STUDIES COURSE?

The Modern Studies course at both Intermediate 1 and 2 has a large amount of choice. The course consists of three sections, and you will study at least one study theme from each section. The content and topics covered are likely to be the same at each level, but, of course, at Intermediate 2 you will go into topics in more depth and detail.

In Section A, Political Issues in the United Kingdom, there is a choice of two study themes: Government and Decision-Making in Scotland, and Government and Decision-Making in Central Government. In Section B, Social Issues in the United Kingdom, there is also a choice of two study themes: Equality in Society: Wealth and Health in the United Kingdom, and Crime and the Law in Society. In Section C, International Issues, there is a choice of five study themes: The Republic of South Africa, The People's Republic of China, The United States of America, The European Union, and Development in Brazil.

The exam, which comes at the end of the course, shows how successful you have been after all your hard work and studying, and this decides what grade you will achieve. During your course, you will also have to pass unit assessments for each of the three units or topics you are studying. These unit assessments are pass/fail and will appear on your exam certificate, but it is important to try to do as well as you can in each of your unit assessments. While a pass is good enough, don't be content with just a pass – doing as well as possible in each unit assessment is good practice for doing very well in your final exam and scoring the highest possible grade. Always aim as high as possible. The questions you will be given as part of your unit assessment will be unseen to you before the assessment – just like in the final exam. The type of questions you will be given will be very similar to what you will face in the final exam. Your teacher should give you feedback after each assessment to help you improve your mark and develop ways of tackling any weaknesses. This book also aims to help you improve your performance so you can do as well as possible.

The Intermediate 1 and 2 courses cover the same topics and study themes – the difference in the exam is the depth of knowledge and understanding you need to show and how complex the sources are in the Evaluating questions. At Intermediate 1, all the questions are worth 4 marks. At Intermediate 2, a wider range of marks is given: questions can be worth 4 marks, 6 marks or 8 marks, and the Decision-Making Task in the Social Issues section is worth 10 marks.

WHAT IS THE MODERN STUDIES EXAM LIKE?

It is important that you are familiar with the layout of the examination paper and know in advance the study themes that you should answer in the exam. There is a wide choice of topics in the Intermediate course, and therefore the exam paper is quite long. You should not waste time looking at topics you have not studied – go straight to the sections that you have studied in class. The front of the exam paper will list the various study themes and the pages in the exam paper that they are on.

This Examination Paper consists of 3 Sections. Within each Section there is a choice of Study Themes. There is one question for each Study Theme.

Section A – Political Issues in the United Kingdom (answer one question)

Question 1	Study Theme 1A	Government and Decision Making in Scotland	Pages	3 – 7
Question 2	Study Theme 1B	Government and Decision Making in Central Government	Pages	7 – 9

Section B – Social Issues in the United Kingdom (answer one question)

Question 3	Study Theme 2A	Equality in Society: Wealth and Health in the United Kingdom	Pages	15– 17
Question 4	Study Theme 2B	Crime and the Law in Society	Pages	19 – 21

Section C – International Issues (answer one question)

Question 5	Study Theme 3A	The Republic of South Africa	Pages	23 – 25
Question 6	Study Theme 3B	The People's Republic of China	Pages	26 – 27
Question 7	Study Theme 3C	The United States of America	Pages	28 – 29
Question 8	Study Theme 3D	The European Union	Pages	30 – 31
Question 9	Study Theme 3E	Development in Brazil	Pages	32 – 33

You should know from your work in class what study themes you have covered and therefore which questions you should attempt. Before you open up your exam paper, read all the instructions on the front cover carefully. Put a tick beside the **three** questions you are going to do – remember to attempt **only one** from each section. If, during your course, you have studied Government and Decision-Making in Scotland, Crime and the Law in Society and The United States of America, put a tick (✔) beside questions 1, 4 and 7 and make a note of the pages on which these questions start.

This Examination Paper consists of 3 Sections. Within each Section there is a choice of Study Themes. There is one question for each Study Theme.

Section A – Political Issues in the United Kingdom (answer one question)
✔ Question 1   Study Theme 1A   Government and Decision Making in Scotland
   Question 2   Study Theme 1B   Government and Decision Making in Central Government

Section B – Social Issues in the United Kingdom (answer one question)
   Question 3   Study Theme 2A   Equality in Society: Wealth and Health in the United Kingdom
✔ Question 4   Study Theme 2B   Crime and the Law in Society

Section C – International Issues (answer one question)
   Question 5   Study Theme 3A   The Republic of South Africa
   Question 6   Study Theme 3B   The People's Republic of China
✔ Question 7   Study Theme 3C   The United States of America
   Question 8   Study Theme 3D   The European Union
   Question 9   Study Theme 3E   Development in Brazil

Make a note of the topics or study themes you have covered in class. Usually there will be three, although some schools may do more than this. Write down which questions you will attempt in the exam. Check this over before the exam to make sure you do not waste any time in the exam or even answer the wrong question by mistake.

Once you have chosen which questions you are going to answer, remember that each question is divided up into several parts – and you must do **all parts** of each question you have chosen. One of the main reasons for students not achieving their highest possible marks or even in some cases failing the exam is that they do not attempt all the questions. Either missing out a question or part of a question, or not finishing the paper due to lack of time, will seriously reduce your marks. We will come back to time management later in this chapter.

Answer one question from each section – Political Issues, Social Issues and International Issues. Answer every part of the question. Do not go on to the next question until you see a message like this at the bottom of the page:

NOW GO TO SECTION B ON PAGE 11

When answering Knowledge and Understanding questions at Intermediate 1 and 2, you will be expected to show a knowledge and understanding of recent social, political and economic issues in the countries and about the topics you have studied.

Social	Political	Economic
Social issues in Modern Studies refer to issues that affect the way people live their lives and would include an understanding of topics such as health, education, crime and the law, and family structures.	Political issues refer to government and politics and would include topics such as government, political parties, voting, pressure groups, and the influence of the media.	Economic issues relate to money and wealth and would include topics such as employment and unemployment, incomes and wages, wealth and poverty.

Use your notebook to keep a list of **Social, Political** and **Economic** issues or topics for each of the study themes you are studying.

Intermediate 1

The Intermediate 1 exam is worth 60 marks and lasts one and a half hours. The instructions on the front will be like this:

X236/101

NATIONAL QUALIFICATIONS	MODERN STUDIES
	INTERMEDIATE 1

1 Read the questions carefully.
2 You must answer **one** question from **each** of Section A, Section B and Section C.
3 You must answer all parts of the questions you choose.
4 You should spend approximately 30 minutes on each Section.
5 If you cannot do a question or part of a question, move on and try again later.
6 Write your answers in the book provided. Indicate clearly, in the left-hand margin, the question and section of question being answered. Do not write in the right-hand margin.

All the information and advice is important, but you should especially note point 3 at the moment. You must answer each part of the questions you have chosen. At Intermediate 1, there are five parts to each question – a, b, c, d and e.

At Intermediate 1, all the questions (a, b, c, d and e) are worth 4 marks, and each question will usually ask you to make two points in your answer. This makes it fairly straightforward, since the number of marks for a question gives you a guide to how much you should write. We will cover this in more detail in later sections of the book when we look at particular types of question.

The second point to emphasise here is that, in each of the three questions you do (remember **one** Political, **one** Social and **one** International), there are five parts. Each study theme is broken into five 4-mark questions. So, each study theme, in total, is worth 20 marks – each section is as important as the other two. The five parts of the question will be a mixture of Knowledge and Understanding questions, where you must write down what you have learned about the topics you have studied, and Evaluating or source-based questions where you will apply your Modern Studies skills. We will look at all the different kinds of questions you will come across throughout your course and in the exam in the later chapters of the book.

If you have studied Modern Studies at Standard Grade level before your Intermediate course, you will already have practised most of the evaluating skills when you did Enquiry Skills questions.

Since each section has the same number of marks and each has the same number of questions, you should aim to divide your time equally between each section. This gives you about 30 minutes to do each section. If you spend too long on earlier sections in the exam, you may leave yourself short of time for the questions at the end of the paper, forcing you to rush questions or even miss out questions completely. This can seriously disadvantage you – so keep an eye on the clock and divide your time up evenly.

If the exam starts at 9.00 am, you should be finished your first question and onto your second by about 9.30 am, and if you have not started your third question by 10.00 you are running short of time. Ideally, you will have some time left at the end (at least five minutes – preferably a bit more) to look over your answers, check that you have answered all the questions, answered the question as it was asked and not left in any 'careless' mistakes caused by the pressure of the exam.

Intermediate 2

The Intermediate 2 exam is worth 70 marks and lasts two hours. The instructions on the front are almost the same as Intermediate 1, but you will notice that there are slight differences in points three and four:

---

3 **You must answer all parts of the questions you choose. Questions in Section A each have four parts; questions in Sections B and C each have three parts.**

4 You should spend approximately 40 minutes on each Section.

You must answer three questions – one from each section. Since you have two hours, you should spend about 40 minutes on each section. This is a rough guide since, at Intermediate 2, some questions have three parts and one question will have four parts. If the four-part question comes in the last section, you will have to cut down slightly your time spent on the first and second questions to give you enough time to do all parts of the final question and still have time to check over your paper.

The question in Section B (Social Issues) is always divided into three parts. In some years, Section A (Political Issues) will have three parts, and in others the question will have four parts. In some years, Section C (International Issues) will have three parts, and in others the question will have four parts. If the question in Section A is divided into four parts, there will only be three parts in Section C. Read the instructions on the front cover of the exam paper to check what you have to do.

Always make sure that you attempt to answer all parts of each question. The instructions on the front cover of the examination paper will tell you in which section the questions are divided into four parts. Each question will be made up of a mixture of Knowledge and Understanding and Evaluating or source-based questions, which we will look at in later chapters of the book. You should make sure that you have seen SQA past papers before the day of the exam and know what the exam paper looks like.

Another point to note at Intermediate 2 level is that different questions are worth different amounts of marks. The number of marks for a question is a guide to how much you should write in your answer. Obviously, you will expect to spend longer on an 8-mark question than on one which is worth only 4 marks. It is important that you have a look to see how much the question is worth before you start to answer. If a question is only worth 4 marks and you write a fantastic answer worth 8 marks, you will still only be able to score 4 marks but you will have used up valuable time you could use later for a longer and more difficult question. We will look later at how much detail you need to include in your answers to score high marks.

Spend a few minutes, before the exam begins, carefully reading the instructions on the front cover so that you know exactly what you have to do and remind yourself which questions you have to tackle.

Managing your time in the exam

 Managing your time in the exam is very important if you are to achieve the best possible mark. The Intermediate 1 exam is one and a half hours long, and the Intermediate 2 exam is two hours long. You should make sure you have divided up your time to give yourself enough time to answer all questions and each part of the questions. Since individual questions towards the end of the Intermediate 2 paper can be worth as much as 8 marks, if you miss out questions or fail to complete the paper, you will find it difficult to gain a high grade or even pass the examination. It is also good to be able to have some time at the end to be able to go over your paper. Sometimes, under exam pressure, you can make careless mistakes. Giving yourself five or 10 minutes at the end of the exam will allow you to check over your paper – make sure you have answered all of the questions; correct any obvious spelling or grammar mistakes; check that you have answered the question in the way it was asked and done all that the question asks you to do.

If you come across a question that you are not sure about, do not spend a long time trying to work it out – leave a space (or you can write it at the end of your examination booklet, but remember to number it clearly in the margin), but make sure you go back to the question later when you have done all the others, and try it again. Sometimes, especially in a 6- or 8-mark question, you may be able to do part of it but are not happy that you have included all the information that you could. In this situation, write what you can and leave a space so that you can go back later and hopefully be able to add to and complete your answer.

If you make a mistake, simply score through your wrong answer with one clear line and go on to write your correct answer. Do not ever use correction products in your exam, since they will only waste valuable time.

Having a structure to answer questions is a good idea, but be careful not to write too much in introducing questions and not leave enough time for the main part of the answer. We will come back to this in later chapters.

In Knowledge and Understanding questions, especially those which are worth 6 or 8 marks at Intermediate 2, it is useful to have a brief plan for your answer. You may think that you do not have time to spend on writing down a plan under examination conditions; but it could save you time in the end, as it can keep your answer organised, give it more structure and avoid repetition. Your plan should be very brief – a few bullet points of the main points that you will include in your answer.

HOW DO I USE STATISTICAL SOURCES?

The American writer Mark Twain famously said that there are 'lies, damn lies and statistics'. The statistics given in the sources in Modern Studies questions are not lies – but statistics can be interpreted in different ways depending upon your point of view.

The table below gives information about 'Executions in Selected Countries in 2002'. If you are going to use any statistical source, no matter whether it is a table, a pie chart or a bar graph, the first thing you should do is look at the title. This may seem obvious – but, under the pressure of a test or exam, sometimes this basic advice can be overlooked.

SOURCE 2

Title

Number of Executions in Selected Countries, 2002

Country	Number of executions	Number of executions per million people
China	1067	0·82 per million
Democratic Republic of Congo	100	1·76 per million
United States	68	0·23 per million
Iran	66	0·96 per million
Egypt	48	0·64 per million
Belarus	33	3·19 per million
Taiwan	32	1·41 per million

Column headings

Data or information

You should also look at the different column headings. The first is clear; it tells you the countries about which evidence is included in the table. The next two columns are the ones headed 'Number of executions' and 'Number of executions per million people'. Below these headings is the data or information that you will use as evidence in your answer. Although both columns give information about executions, it is presented in different ways.

- The column headed 'Number of executions' shows the actual number of people executed in different countries in 2002. According to these figures, China had by far the highest number of executions, at 1067, compared with the next highest, Democratic Republic of Congo, which executed 100 people, and Taiwan, which had the lowest number of executions at 32. So, if you wanted to show that China was very harsh in executing criminals, then you would use these figures in your answer.

- The column headed 'Number of executions per million people' also gives figures for executions but presents them in a different way. Here, executions are given as a rate rather than as an absolute number. This is a common way of presenting information and allows comparisons to be made between populations of different sizes. You will be used to seeing information being presented as a rate – for example, many statistics are presented as a percentage (%), which means per hundred. Other figures, such as infant mortality rates, are usually shown as a figure per thousand. The example above gives the rate per million. Using this column, it is not China which has the highest figure for executions but Belarus. This is because, even though Belarus executed only 33 people compared to China's figure of over 1000, Belarus's rate of executions per million was 3·19 while China's was only 0·82. The reason for the difference is of course that China has a huge population of over 1000 million while the population of Belarus is less than 10 million. By comparing the countries in the table, China has the fifth highest rate of executions, since four other countries all have a higher rate and only the USA and Egypt have a lower rate. If you wish to oppose the view that China is harsh in its treatment of criminals, it is these figures you would use, by pointing out that China has a lower rate of executions compared to several other countries, for example, Belarus.

Be very careful, when using statistics in your answer, that you refer to them accurately. There is a huge difference between saying that 'in China there were 0·82 million executions' and 'in China the rate of executions is 0·82 per million'. The first example is completely inaccurate and would give a huge figure. Always check carefully the way in which statistics are presented. Think about the way you use the statistics, and read them over when you are checking your answer to see that what you have written makes sense.

WILL THIS BOOK GIVE ME THE CONTENT I NEED FOR THE EXAM?

The main purpose of this book is not to give you a large amount of content to include in exam questions. You will be given plenty of information about the topics you are studying by your teacher or lecturer. You will have notes from class, you will use textbooks, you will see TV programmes and documentaries, you will read newspapers and magazines and you will probably have access to vast amounts of information on the Internet.

Although there will be information in some of the questions and example answers contained here, the main purpose of this book is to give you the skills and techniques to answer questions and use your knowledge effectively.

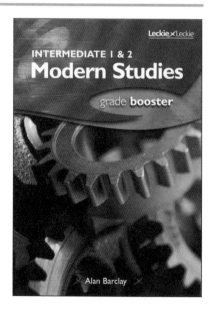

WHAT IS IN THIS BOOK?

The first two chapters of this book deal with how to answer the different kinds of Knowledge and Understanding questions at both Intermediate 1 and 2. You will find out the difference between questions which ask you to describe and questions which ask you to explain and give reasons.

The third and fourth chapters of the book give you skills to answer all the different kinds of Evaluating questions. Evaluating questions have sources which you must use to make comparisons, support or oppose a point of view, make decisions, draw conclusions and explain exaggeration or selectivity in the use of facts. Just as with any skill, the more you practise it the better you will get at it. This book attempts to give you practice in the Modern Studies skills which you need to be successful.

Some of the questions you will see in this book will not be on topics that are familiar to you. Don't panic. It may be that you will study the topic later in the course, or the question is on one of the study themes that your school or college does not cover. However, the advice given can be applied to whatever topics you actually are studying. Throughout the book, we will cover all of the topics that most schools and colleges do study.

Remember that no one book is the answer to doing well. This book will help you, but it is part of a package. Paying attention and working hard in class are important. Listen to the advice given to you by your teacher or lecturer. Do regular revision. Spend enough time on any homework activities you are given. Before important unit assessments and exams, make sure you go over all your notes. Keep your notes and books well organised.

Modern Studies is an ever-changing subject – there will always be something about the topics you are studying on television news, in newspapers and on the Internet. It doesn't take a large amount of time to keep up to date, and it can make a huge difference to how well you will do in Modern Studies.

1 Answering Knowledge and Understanding Questions at Intermediate 1

Introduction

How to answer 'describe' questions at Intermediate 1

How to answer 'explain' questions at Intermediate 1

INTRODUCTION

In both Intermediate 1 and Intermediate 2 papers, Knowledge and Understanding (KU) questions will make up about half of the marks available. These questions are set to allow you to show some of what you have learned during your Modern Studies course. Throughout your course, you will have gained a wide understanding of political, social and international issues. Of course, in the exam you will not be asked to write about everything you have learned. The exam can only ever sample a small part of what you have studied. However, since you do not know exactly what will be asked in the exam, you must make sure you have revised thoroughly and are prepared for whatever questions may be asked. The exam is your chance to show what you know.

There are two aspects to doing well in this type of question:

- First, paying attention in class, working hard, revising regularly, reading your textbooks, studying the *Intermediate Course Notes*, using the Internet, reading newspapers and watching news programmes and documentaries on television.

Make up your own diagram to show different ways you can develop your own knowledge and understanding of Modern Studies topics.

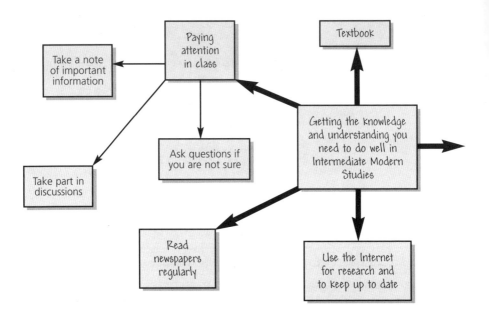

- Secondly, it is no use having all this information if you let yourself down by not answering the questions in the most effective way. The purpose of this chapter is to help you present what you know in the most effective way and to demonstrate your understanding of the Modern Studies topics that you have studied.

There are two types of KU questions. The first type are questions which ask you to **describe** a political, social or international issue, while the second type of question asks you to give **explanations**, show what has caused something to happen or give a balanced argument. In general, explain-type questions are more difficult and require you to show what causes things to happen. If you give answers to this type of question which only describe and provide no explanation, you will gain few if any marks.

The number of marks for each question is a good guide to how much you should write in your answers. At Intermediate 1, all the questions are worth 4 marks, so you need to make two points in your answer. At Intermediate 2, Knowledge and Understanding questions can be worth 4, 6 or 8 marks. For 4 marks, two points must be made in order to score full marks, although up to 3 marks can be awarded for a well-developed, high-quality point with supporting examples. It is recommended that, in 6-mark questions, three points should be made and developed, and in 8-mark questions you should attempt to make four developed points.

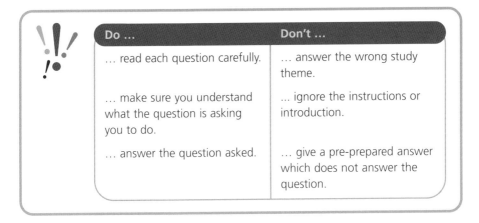

Do ...	Don't ...
... read each question carefully.	... answer the wrong study theme.
... make sure you understand what the question is asking you to do.	... ignore the instructions or introduction.
... answer the question asked.	... give a pre-prepared answer which does not answer the question.

At both Intermediate 1 and 2, questions may address quite specific issues, and you need to bring relevant and reasonably recent knowledge to your answers. In your revision, you should make sure that you have a range of knowledge which is relevant and up to date. Some answers suffer, especially in certain international topics, from being too historical and using information which is not up to date. Knowledge can also often be one-sided and presented in an exaggerated way and this will not gain many marks.

Answering Intermediate 1 Knowledge and Understanding questions

The first thing to remember about questions at Intermediate 1 is that they are all worth 4 marks. This means that you must make two points in your answer to score full marks. While this section will help you to present the information and knowledge you have in order to score as many marks as possible, you have to have the knowledge and understanding in the first place. Some of the questions and sample answers in the sections which follow may not be familiar to you. Don't worry – they may not be topics you have studied. However, the points about how to answer the questions apply equally to all the topics in the course.

HOW TO ANSWER 'DESCRIBE' QUESTIONS AT INTERMEDIATE 1

This type of question is asking you to show your knowledge and understanding of a topic which you have studied and to write down that information. You may have studied some of the topics in class several months before, so revision before any assessment or exam is essential if you are to do well.

Look at the following question (SQA 2006) and the sample answers which follow.

EXAM EXAMPLE 1

> *Intermediate 1, 2006 paper, question 2(a)*
>
> **Pressure groups use a variety of methods to influence decision-making.**
>
> **Describe two methods pressure groups use to influence decision-making.**   (4 marks)

This is a weak answer.

The first method pressure groups will use to influence decision-making is to hold a demonstration and the second method is to have a petition.

Why is this a weak answer?

This answer makes two correct points, mentioning both 'a demonstration' and 'a petition', which are two of the most common methods used by pressure groups. However, neither point is described in any way that shows that the person who has written the answer actually knows what a demonstration or a petition is. This answer would be treated as a *list* and would not gain many marks. This answer also could go on to make extra points about lobbying, letter-writing campaigns and boycotting but would still not gain any extra marks if none of them was explained.

This is a good answer, but could be improved.

The first method pressure groups will use to influence decision-making is to hold a demonstration. This is where large numbers of people protest on the streets with banners.

The second method is to have a petition where the pressure group gets as many people as possible to sign a petition sheet that says they agree with the aims of the pressure group.

Why is this a better answer?

This is a much better answer, since it still makes the two correct points about 'demonstration' and 'petition' but the answer shows understanding of what each of the two methods involves. Each of the two points is developed with some detail. This answer would score high marks. So, each part of this answer makes a point (P) and goes on to give some description by explaining (E) what each point means.

This answer is also good because it has separated the two points in the answer into different paragraphs and uses a style of answer which makes sure that two points are mentioned in the answer by saying, 'The first method pressure groups will use …' and 'The second method …' without using too many words and using up too much valuable time.

This is a very good answer.

The first method pressure groups will use to influence decision-making is to hold a demonstration. This is where large numbers of people protest on the streets with banners. For example, many hundreds of thousands of people joined demonstrations against the war in Iraq.

The second method is to have a petition where they get as many people as possible to sign a petition sheet that says they agree with the aims of the pressure group. For example, almost two million people signed an e-petition to the government against road tolls.

Why is this a very good answer?

This is an excellent answer which adds examples to the earlier answer. This answer shows knowledge of two different methods and can describe them, but goes on to show real understanding by being able to link relevant and reasonably recent examples to the methods.

You are writing Modern Studies answers – your examples should therefore not be too historical. They should be reasonably up to date. As a guide, giving examples from the twenty-first century, i.e. from 2000 onwards, should be fine. Your teacher and recent textbooks will give you relevant examples you can include in your answers. Your own reading of newspapers and use of the Internet will provide you with more good examples.

In summary, each part of the third answer makes a correct point (P), gives some explanation (E) and then links it with a relevant example (E).

P Point   make your point briefly

E Explain   give a more detailed description/explanation of your point

E Example give an up-to-date example to support your point

Answer the 2006 question on pressure groups. Use two points not used in the sample answer, giving description and examples for each point.

When answering questions in the International Issues section, it is very important that you are able to show you are writing about the country you have studied. Some answers are too vague and general and could be referring to anywhere. This problem is often seen in questions on the United States of America.

Look at the following question from the 2007 SQA exam paper.

EXAM EXAMPLE 2

Intermediate 1, 2007 paper, question 7(a)

People in the USA can take part in politics in many ways.
Describe two ways people in the USA can take part in politics.
(4 marks)

This is a good answer, but could be improved.

The first way people in the USA can take part in politics is by making sure they are registered to vote and then actually going out to vote on election day.

The second way someone can take part in politics in the USA is by joining a political party and helping out during an election campaign by offering to take people to the polling station or phoning up voters to persuade them to vote.

Why is this a good answer?

In many ways, this is a good answer. The first point is about 'voting' and is developed slightly by saying 'making sure they are registered to vote ...'. The second point about 'joining a political party' is also correct and is very well developed by giving two relevant descriptions of what a party member might do to help in a campaign. However, there is nothing in the answer which shows it is about the United States of America rather than Britain, and therefore it would not get full marks.

This is where suitable examples can be used. In the first paragraph, the following sentence can be added in order to show that your knowledge about political participation is being applied to an American situation:

 For example, people in the USA can vote for their President every four years.

In the second paragraph, including the following example would complete the answer:

 In the USA, the two main parties that most people support and vote for are the Democrats and the Republicans.

Either of these examples would be enough to make sure the answer receives full marks – and neither of them involves a large amount of extra writing or would take up much time.

 Using examples. Giving up-to-date and relevant examples is very important in your answer. The USA has a President, not a Prime Minister, so that is a good example to use, since it shows you have an understanding of US politics. In the USA, they refer to 'pressure groups' as 'interest groups'. The main parties in the USA are the Democrats and the Republicans. Do not write about MPs or MSPs in USA questions – they have Senators and Congressmen and Congresswomen.

Answer the USA question describing two other ways that people in the USA can take part in politics – remember to give examples from the USA in your answer.

HOW TO ANSWER 'EXPLAIN' QUESTIONS AT INTERMEDIATE 1

In this type of answer, you have to do more than just remember facts and give information that you have learned. In this type of question, your answer must explain a topic by giving reasons for something, or explain an issue by giving reasons for and against something. You are being asked what causes something to happen rather than just describing something that may have happened.

If we look at a question on pressure groups again, you will be able to see how the answer to this type of question is different from the answer given to the question about pressure groups shown earlier.

EXAM EXAMPLE 3

> **Some pressure groups are prepared to break the law in their campaigns.**
>
> **Give *two* reasons why some pressure groups are prepared to break the law in their campaigns.** (4 marks)

This is a weak answer.

Some pressure groups are prepared to break the law by breaking into buildings and climbing onto private property.

This answer tries to make two points – and, while it is true that some pressure groups will break into buildings and climb onto private property, this does not answer the question. It does not say why they use these methods which break the law. It only describes two ways in which they might break the law, but there is no explanation given.

This is a very good answer.

One reason why some pressure groups are prepared to break the law by breaking into buildings is <u>because</u> they feel that this kind of direct action is the only way they can achieve their aims. For example, animal-rights campaigners have broken into mink farms and released the animals into the wild to achieve their aim of helping animals.

Some pressure groups climb onto private property. They do this <u>so that</u> they will be noticed and get a lot of publicity. For example, Fathers4Justice have climbed onto the balcony of Buckingham Palace with their banners, and their actions were shown on television to millions of people.

Why is this a very good answer?

This answer is much better, since it does tackle the question in the correct way by giving two reasons for the pressure groups using illegal methods. This type of answer uses words and phrases such as **'because'**, **'so that'**, **'in order to'** and **'so'** in order to give the explanation. Again, each part of the answer gives an example to back up the explanation given.

In the following question from the Social Issues section, it would be easy to give a 'describe' answer rather than give reasons.

EXAM EXAMPLE 4

> **Some people in Scotland suffer from poor health.**
>
> **Give *two* reasons why some people in Scotland suffer from poor health.**
> (4 marks)

It would be easy to list several
descriptions of poor health in Scotland:

- High rate of heart disease
- Obesity
- High level of lung cancer
- Men usually die earlier than women
- High level of illness in some parts of
  large cities, e.g. parts of Glasgow,
  Dundee and Edinburgh

Each of these points does describe the poor health situation of some people in
Scotland but of course, on their own, they do not give any reasons or explanation.
You can use any two of these points to give a correct answer as shown below.

This is a good answer.

One health problem some people in Scotland face is a high level of heart
disease. One reason for the high level of heart disease in Scotland is a poor
diet. Many people in Scotland eat a lot of high-fat foods rather than fresh
fruit and vegetables.

A second health problem in Scotland is that, in some parts of large cities,
people suffer from more illness. A reason for some areas having more illness
is that these areas suffer from more poverty. People who are poorer may
have to live in damp houses, which can lead to breathing difficulties.

Why is this a good answer?

This answer gives two explanations. You do have to use your knowledge of the
health problems faced by some people, but your answer must go on to say what
causes these problems. This shows that you have a deeper knowledge and
understanding of Modern Studies issues than when you simply describe.

In the second Social Issues topic, Crime and the Law in Society, the following
question could be asked.

EXAM EXAMPLE 5

> **There are many reasons why some young people commit crime.**
>
> **Give *two* reasons why some young people commit crime.** (4 marks)

Again, your starting point could be some of the crimes most commonly committed by younger people:

- Vandalism
- Shoplifting
- 'Joy riding'
- Assault

In this answer, you must go on to explain why some young people may commit any of these crimes.

- Choose either of the questions from the Social Issues section – about reasons for poorer health or reasons for committing crime.
- Answer the question using **two** of the bullet points given, and explain why
  - some people in Scotland suffer from poorer health, or
  - some young people commit crime.

In the International Issues section, it is important that your information and explanations are up to date.

EXAM EXAMPLE 6

Intermediate 1, 2006 paper, question 8(c)

People in China have benefited from economic reforms. (2006)

Give *two* reasons why people in China have benefited from economic reforms. (4 marks)

This is a very good answer.

One way in which people in China have benefited from economic reforms is that people are now allowed to own businesses. If their business is successful, it will make profit which the owners will be able to spend on luxury goods. For example, rich people in China can buy luxury cars.

A second way in which people have benefited from economic reform is that China has become more open in recent years. By holding the Olympic Games in China in 2008, many new buildings and sporting facilities will be built. Many people will be better off, as they will get jobs in the building industry and they will be able to earn wages.

Why is this a very good answer?

This answer shows knowledge and understanding of the economic reforms in China which have allowed people to own their own businesses and made the Chinese economy more open. Each point goes on to explain how these reforms have benefited people. The reference to the Olympic Games is a very up-to-date example.

Answering Knowledge and Understanding Questions at Intermediate 2

Introduction

How to answer 'describe' questions at Intermediate 2

How to answer 'explain' questions at Intermediate 2

INTRODUCTION

The basic points we have discussed about answering Knowledge and Understanding questions at Intermediate 1 also apply to answering Intermediate 2 questions. The first main difference is that Intermediate 2 questions may sometimes ask about less obvious topics, although you should not be asked any questions that you have not studied in class. The second difference is that Intermediate 2 questions are not all out of 4 marks. In an Intermediate 2 paper, you will find Knowledge and Understanding questions worth 4 marks, 6 marks and 8 marks.

About half of the 70 marks in the paper will be made up of Knowledge and Understanding questions, so it is important to have both the information and the understanding that you will include in your answer. You should also practise the techniques for answering the questions in order to best display your knowledge.

There are various ways to remember to give detailed explanations in your answers.

P   Point   make your point briefly

E   Explain   give a detailed and well-developed explanation/description of your point

E   Example   give up-to-date examples to support your point

You should make a point (P), describe or explain (E) the point further and provide relevant examples (E) to support the description or explanation given. Individual points made, without any detailed development or explanation, no matter how accurate or how many you make, will be treated as a *list* and given a maximum of only 2 marks.

HOW TO ANSWER 'DESCRIBE' QUESTIONS AT INTERMEDIATE 2

The following example shows how to answer a question from the 2007 exam paper. You should notice that Intermediate 2 questions contain the words 'in detail'. This indicates that you are expected to develop your answers more fully at this level than at Intermediate 1.

EXAM EXAMPLE 1

Intermediate 2, 2007 paper, question 1(a)

MSPs can represent their constituents in the Scottish Parliament in a number of ways.

Describe, *in detail*, *two* ways MSPs can represent their constituents in the Scottish Parliament.   (4 marks)

This is a good answer.

One way MSPs can represent their constituents in the Scottish Parliament is by asking a question to a Cabinet Secretary at Question Time about a topic their constituents are concerned about. This usually takes place each week when the Parliament is sitting, when ministers

answer MSPs' questions. The MSP can ask the Education Minister a question about schools in their area, since this is a devolved matter.

A second way an MSP can represent their constituents is to try to bring in a new law that the people in their area want. An MSP can introduce a Member's Bill; for example, the Scottish Parliament banned fox-hunting with dogs after an MSP introduced a Bill.

Why is this a good answer?

Each paragraph in this answer makes a point about asking questions and passing laws. Description is given with some detail to show understanding. An example of a law passed after being introduced by an MSP is given. Since this question is worth only 4 marks, there is enough in this sample answer to get full marks. The examples we will look at in the rest of this section will be worth 6 marks or 8 marks.

Read the question carefully. This question asks how an MSP can represent their constituents in the Scottish Parliament. You would not use examples from the constituency work of MSPs such as holding surgeries, since this is not what the question is asking you to describe.

In the Social Issues section, Study Theme 2A: Equality in Society: Wealth and Health in the United Kingdom, you may be asked questions on either wealth-related topics or health-related topics, or in some cases questions may allow you to refer to both.

The next question refers to health care and is from the 2007 paper.

EXAM EXAMPLE 2

Intermediate 2, 2007 paper, question 3(a)

The National Health Service in Scotland provides both primary and secondary health care services.

Describe, *in detail*, primary and secondary health care services provided by the NHS in Scotland. (6 marks)

The National Health Service is a massive organisation, responsible for meeting the health needs of the population of the UK. It provides a very wide range of health care services, many of which you will have learned about in class, and you are also likely to have personal experience of some health care services yourself. Remember that, since Modern Studies refers to real-life situations going on in the UK and other parts of the world, you will be able to bring your own personal knowledge to add to your understanding of the topics you study in class.

The question tries to help you by mentioning that you can include examples of 'primary' and 'secondary' services. At Intermediate 2 level, you should be aware of what these terms mean.

Primary health care services usually refer to family doctor (GP) services but would also include dental services, optical services, prescriptions and mental health services. Secondary health care is usually focused on hospital care and will include acute services, geriatric care of the elderly in a hospital situation, maternity care and so on.

Since this question is worth 6 marks, you should aim to make three developed points in your answer and give examples.

This is a very good answer.

One service provided by the National Health Service is the family doctor service. If people are ill, they will usually go to their doctor first of all. The doctor may examine them and diagnose what is wrong with them and prescribe medication. This service is free of charge under the NHS.

A second service provided by the NHS is accident and emergency (A&E) treatment. If someone is seriously injured in a car accident, they may be taken to an A&E centre where they will receive immediate treatment which may save their life. Doctors and nurses work in these centres to provide health care services for whoever needs it.

The third health care service is maternity care. The NHS will provide ante-natal care during a woman's pregnancy such as regular check-ups and advice on keeping the baby healthy. The birth will probably take place in an NHS hospital with midwives in attendance; and, after the baby is born, a community midwife will visit the mother and baby at home.

Why is this a very good answer?

This is not a complicated answer and mentions three well-known health care services. There are many others that could have been included in the answer. It does, however, use some specialist terms which show the sort of knowledge of this topic which would be expected at this level, for example 'diagnose', 'prescribe', 'ante-natal' and 'midwife'. These are the sort of terms which you are bound to have come across when studying this topic and which you should include in your answer to display the knowledge you have of this topic.

> To help you remember the specific words and phrases that you come across in Modern Studies and which are so useful in answering questions, keep a note in the back of a jotter or in a notebook of words you come across in Modern Studies and their meanings.

Obviously, the questions in the exam papers will change each year. It is not possible to ask the same questions for each topic year after year. So, while it is very good advice to look over past papers and practise lots of exam questions from past papers, you must be prepared to answer whatever question is set – NOT only the questions you have practised and would want to answer. If you try to '*turn*' a question around from the one that is in the paper to the one you would like to answer and may have done a lot of work preparing for, you are unlikely to get many marks, if any at all.

You must also be prepared to answer a range of questions and be careful not to adopt a one-sided and stereotypical approach to the topic studied which gives an exaggerated or overly simple view of the topic. It is also important to read the question carefully in order to understand exactly what the question is asking.

EXAM EXAMPLE 3

> *Intermediate 2, 2007 paper, question 6(a)*
>
> **There are opportunities for political participation and representation in China. (2007)**
>
> **Describe, *in detail*, the opportunities for political participation and representation in China.**   (6 marks)

Some students may assume that any question about political participation and representation in China must be about limitations and restrictions – but this question asks about opportunities for political participation and representation. Turning the question around to list restrictions would not gain marks.

Some people answered this question in the following way.

This is a poor answer.

There is no chance for political participation in China as there is only one political party, the Communist Party. People in China are never allowed to vote in elections. In China, people are not allowed to protest, as if they do they will be killed like in Tiananmen Square, where thousands of students were killed for protesting for more freedom.

Why is this a poor answer?

The approach of this answer does not reflect the question that was asked. The answer does refer to information that has probably been learned in class or from a textbook, but has a number of problems:

❶ It refers only to the lack of political participation and does not refer to any of the opportunities for political involvement in China, which, although they may be limited, do exist.

❷ The answer makes some factual errors; for example, there are political parties other than the Communist Party now legal in China, and Chinese people now do have a limited right to vote in local elections.

❸ The answer makes reference to the Tiananmen Square massacre. This took place in 1989 and, while being a very important event, is now rather dated to use as an example in a Modern Studies answer.

A correct approach could be as follows.

This is a very good answer.

People in China can participate in politics by joining the Communist Party of China (CPC). The Communist Party is the main political party in China and is in control of the government of China. An example of participation is that members will encourage voters to go out and vote for CPC candidates in village elections.

At a younger age, young people can join the Young Communist Youth League. This will give young people experience of politics in China and give them a better chance of joining the CPC when they are older. They can participate by spreading the ideas of the Communist Party among the people of China.

People in China have a right to vote at the local level. Village committees are elected every three years. They are responsible for the administration of the village and health services in the village.

Why is this a very good answer?

This answer makes three detailed points. It gives three ways in which Chinese people have some opportunities to participate in the political system: joining the Communist Party of China, joining the Young Communist Youth League and voting in village elections. Each point is explained, and examples are given to support the explanation. It also does not rely on examples from before 2000, so is a more up-to-date and modern answer.

HOW TO ANSWER 'EXPLAIN' QUESTIONS AT INTERMEDIATE 2

As was the case with Intermediate 1 questions of this type, you must do more than just describe information. In answering this type of question, you must give explanations. With Intermediate 2 questions of this type, questions may be worth 4 marks but are more likely to be worth either 6 or 8 marks. The questions at Intermediate 2 may require you to answer about more complex or less obvious issues, but, again, you are very unlikely to be asked about something you have not studied in class.

This question appeared in the 2007 paper, before the formation of the minority SNP government following the election in May 2007.

EXAM EXAMPLE 4

> *Intermediate 2, 2007 paper, question 1(b)*
>
> **The Scottish Executive has been made up of a coalition of two parties since 1999.**
>
> **Explain, *in detail*, why some people believe a coalition is a good way of governing Scotland.** (6 marks)

P
E
E

This is a very good answer.

A coalition is a government which is made up of more than one party. Some people think that a coalition is a good way of governing Scotland because more voters will feel that the government represents them, therefore it is more democratic. For example, in the Labour and Liberal

Democrat coalition, people who voted Labour and people who voted Lib Dem will be able to support the government.

A coalition government is fairer <u>because</u> more people will have voted for it. Coalition is usually found where there is proportional representation. Under 'first past the post', you do not need over half of the votes to win a majority – usually under PR you do need over half of the votes to win over half of the seats. Coalition government means that a party that has not won half of the votes cannot win over half of the seats in the Scottish Parliament. For example, Labour and Liberal Democrats together won over half the votes and over half the seats.

Coalition government is also good <u>because</u> it means that parties have to discuss issues and compromise. A majority government may only put forward its own policies, which most people may not agree with. The parties in a coalition will only put forward policies that both parties agree to. For example, the coalition in Scotland discussed university fees and agreed that there would be fees for attending university, but they compromised by saying they would be paid after students had graduated.

Why is this a very good answer?

This answer begins by giving a brief definition of 'coalition government'. This starts the answer off well by showing that the candidate understands what the question is about. The first point uses the word 'because', showing that the answer is explaining rather than just describing. It then goes on to give an example about the Labour and Liberal Democrat coalition in Scotland up until 2007.

In the second paragraph of the answer, it is mentioned that coalition government tends to come about in proportional-representation systems. This is where it is important not to 'turn' the question and start describing voting systems, which is not what the question is about. Keep the focus on coalition government. This point explains the advantage of coalition in terms of the disadvantages of other system. This is one way of answering the question but needs to done carefully in case you move away from what the question is asking. However, it is valid to say 'coalition government is good because majority (or minority) government of one party has problems', and then go on to explain what these problems could be.

The final point again contrasts coalition with majority government and explains that, under coalition, parties will be more likely to compromise, and gives an example from Scotland of student fees being discussed and an agreement being reached between the coalition partners.

In 2007, the SNP won the largest number of seats in the election to the Scottish Parliament. They formed a minority government. One of their first acts was to rename the 'Scottish Executive' as the 'Scottish Government'. From 2008, the term Scottish Government will be used in Modern Studies questions, but you may still come across the former name in past-paper questions.

The following question is worth 8 marks and is from the 2007 exam.

EXAM EXAMPLE 5

Intermediate 2, 2007 paper, question 3(b)

Reducing poverty in the United Kingdom is an important government policy.

Explain, *in detail*, why reducing poverty in the United Kingdom is an important government policy. (8 marks)

This is a good answer – first part only.

The first reason why reducing poverty is an important government policy is <u>because</u> being poor is linked to poor health. People who live in poverty are more likely to suffer illness and die at an earlier age than people who are well off. For example, poorer people will have less money to spend on a healthy diet, so they may eat cheaper and less healthy food, leading to poorer health.

A second reason why the government wants to reduce poverty is <u>because</u> it would cut the amount the government spends on benefits. People who are poor will receive income support and free school meals, and this costs a lot of money. If there are fewer poor people, the government will be able to spend less on benefits and cut taxes.

These two paragraphs partly answer the question – if you are studying this topic, you can complete the question to bring it up to a full 8-mark answer. (See activity on the next page.)

This topic covers Wealth and Health. Questions may refer to wealth only, or health only, or, as in the first paragraph above, you can link wealth and health together.

Knowledge and Understanding questions may be worth up to 8 marks. You should give yourself a short time to plan out an answer before you begin writing in order to be clear about what you are going to say. Keep your answer organised and avoid repeating yourself. Because time is short in the exam, any plan should be very brief. Three or four bullet points giving the main points you will develop in your answer is as much as you should include in your plan.

Intermediate 2, 2007 paper, question 4(b)

There are many reasons why some people commit crime.

Explain, *in detail*, why some people commit crime.   (8 marks)

You should aim to make four developed points in a question which is worth 8 marks.

You could include a small 'spider' diagram or a list of bullet points before you begin writing. You would than have to develop each point in more detail and give examples to support your explanations.

Spider diagram

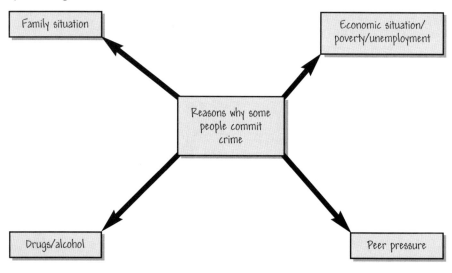

Government aims to reduce poverty:

- Poverty causes poor health
- Reduce government spending on benefits
- Impact on children, e.g. do less well in school
- Strain on family may increase divorce

> Choose either of the Social Issues questions on reducing poverty or reasons for crime.
>
> Answer the question, making developed points and giving relevant examples to support your answer.

> In the International Issues section of the examination, you will not be given marks for knowledge which is too historical. For example, in the study theme about South Africa, descriptions of what life was like under Apartheid will not gain marks; in the study theme on China, if you write about the protests which took place in Tiananmen Square in 1989, you will not score marks.

> *Intermediate 2, 2007 paper, question 5(b)*
>
> **The Government of South Africa faces political opposition from various groups.**
>
> **Explain, *in detail*, why the Government of South Africa faces political opposition from various groups.**　(6 marks)

This is a very good answer – first developed point only.

One reason why the South African Government faces political opposition is because the South African government is dominated by the African National Congress, which has over two thirds of the members in the National Assembly. The ANC is mostly supported by Black African voters, and most of the government ministers are Black. Some White South Africans think that the government is not concerned about them and that its policies are to support Black South Africans.

This is the first part of the answer and gives one reason; if you have covered the study theme on South Africa, you should now go on and try to give up-to-date explanations and examples of two more points to complete the answer to this question.

3 Answering Evaluating Questions at Intermediate 1

Evaluating Skills at Intermediate 1 Modern Studies

Differences

Support and oppose a point of view

Decision-making

Conclusions

Exaggeration

In Knowledge and Understanding questions, you are asked to show what you have learned in class or from your own work, studying books, revising your notes and using informative websites on the Internet. You are asked to describe what you know about the topics you have studied or to explain issues.

Evaluating questions are different. You are given sources to study, and you must use the **skills** you have learned and practised in Modern Studies to show differences, draw conclusions, make decisions and so on. You may have practised most of the Evaluating skills you will use at Intermediate if you did Standard Grade Modern Studies – at Standard Grade, they are known as enquiry skills.

EVALUATING SKILLS AT INTERMEDIATE 1 MODERN STUDIES

Just like the Knowledge and Understanding questions at Intermediate 1, all the Evaluating questions are also worth **4** marks each. This makes things simpler, since you do not need to spend time looking at the number of marks and deciding how much to write. Each question will usually tell you that you should do two things in order to get full marks.

In Intermediate 1 questions, there will usually be fewer sources (either one or two), and the information in the sources will be more straightforward and easier to understand than the sources in Intermediate 2 questions. You should get used to using different kinds of sources because the information can be presented in different ways:

- Written information
- Factfiles
- Pictures
- Tables
- Pie charts
- Line graphs
- Bar graphs

In this section of the book, you will see how to use each of these different types of source. Some questions will contain a mixture of sources presenting the information in different ways.

DIFFERENCES

In this type of question, you are given two sources. This information may be in the form of two written sources giving different information or opinions about an issue, information in the form of tables with figures, or pictures. We will look at examples of each type of question.

When answering this type of question, you are usually looking at different people's opinions about the same thing – in some parts they may agree, so there are no differences, but in other parts they may disagree, so there are differences in their point of view or in the information being given.

Imagine two football fans, who each support different teams, going to the same match. The final score is City 1, United 0. At the end of the 90 minutes, both fans agree that the score was 1-0 to City. However, they may disagree about the goal. The City fan thinks that his team scored a superb goal, with their new striker scoring a brilliant header from a cross. The United fan may have a very different view of the goal. He thinks that the City striker was offside and that the goal should never have been allowed. From where he was sitting, he may believe that the referee never saw that the goal-scorer was offside and that United have been treated unfairly.

So, although both fans have been to the same football match, they have different views about the only goal that was scored.

In the question below (from the 2007 paper), the two sources give different views about immigration into the USA.

EXAM EXAMPLE 1

Intermediate 1, 2007 paper, question 7(c)

Study Sources 1 and 2 below, then answer the question which follows.

Source 1	Source 2
Immigration and the USA	**Immigration into America**
America should have open borders. It is immigration that has made the USA the successful country it is today.	Many immigrants are coming into America from poor countries such as Mexico.
Immigrants come to America to work, and they will often do the jobs that other Americans do not want to do.	Immigrants are attracted to America's wealth and the rights and freedoms that Americans enjoy.
Immigrants want to come to America because it is a wealthy country and its citizens enjoy many human rights. ❶ ❷	Immigration causes unemployment as the new arrivals take jobs from the people who already live in the USA.
Most recent immigrants have come from poor countries like Mexico in order to improve their lives.	It is time America closed its borders otherwise more and more immigration will result in major problems for the country.

> **Sources 1 and 2 give different views about immigration into the USA.**
>
> **Study the two views and write down what these *differences* are.**
>
> **Mention *two* differences in your answer.**
>
> **Your answer must be based entirely on Sources 1 and 2 above.**
>
> (4 marks)

In this question, the two sources each consist of four paragraphs. Two of the paragraphs in Source A are broadly the same as two paragraphs in Source B, while two paragraphs in each give different views. It is these different views that you must find and write down in your answer. The arrows show which paragraphs have different views.

The first thing to do to answer this type of question successfully is to make sure you have carefully read what the question is asking you to do – in this case, write down two differences between the sources about **immigration into the USA.**

Then you must read each of the sources carefully and find the paragraphs where they are writing about the same thing. You should look for the same words or phrases being used in the two different sources. For example, Source 1, paragraph 4 uses the words and phrases 'poor countries' and 'Mexico'; Source 2, paragraph 1 also uses these same words, so you should compare these two paragraphs. In this case, they agree – both are saying that most/many immigrants come from 'poor countries' like/such as 'Mexico'. These two paragraphs from the different sources give very similar views; therefore they are not different and should not be included in your answer.

You must use the information in the sources to show that you have compared the different paragraphs and found where they are not giving the same view and are therefore different. You must include information that has been taken from the sources to show that you have understood the points being made in the sources.

You should always answer the question by giving the first difference, using information from one source, and comparing it with information taken from the other source; then giving a second difference with information from each of the sources. You should not copy out the whole paragraph, but you should paraphrase the most important information from each source to show clearly the differences.

This is a weak answer.

The first difference is open and closed borders.

Why is this a weak answer?

Although this answer has correctly seen that the first paragraph in Source 1 contains a different view about America's borders compared with Source 2, it does not use enough of the information to get full marks.

This is a better answer.

The first difference about immigration into the USA is where Source 1 says that America should have open borders <u>but</u> Source 2 <u>disagrees</u> and says America should have closed borders.

Why is this a better answer?

This is a short answer but gives a clear difference between the two sources and mentions where each piece of information comes from.

It uses words such as '**but**' and '**disagrees**' to show that the views are different. Other words and phrases such as '**however**' or '**on the other hand**' could also be used to show contrasts.

To finish off the answer:

The second difference is that Source 1 says that immigrants come to America to work and they do the jobs that other Americans will not do, so they do not cause unemployment for Americans. <u>On the other hand</u>, Source 2 says that immigrants cause unemployment because they take jobs from people already in the USA.

This part of the answer gives more detail than the first difference. It uses the words from each of the different paragraphs but rearranges them, keeping the main points without changing their meaning but, at the same time, pointing out the different views.

In the above example, the sources were written and the two views were presented side by side. In the example which follows, from the 2007 paper, two General Election results are given. The information is mostly in the form of figures, and the sources are presented one below the other. However, the skill of comparing the two sets of information, and finding and then describing the two differences, remains the same.

EXAM EXAMPLE 2

Intermediate 1, 2007 paper, question 2(e)

Study Sources 1 and 2 below, then answer the question which follows.

Results of the UK General Election in the Western Isles (Na h-Eileanan an Iar)
Constituency: 2001 and 2005

SOURCE 1 2001 UK General Election		
Candidate	Number of votes	Percentage of votes
Calum MacDonald (Labour)	5924	45·0%
Alasdair Nicholson (SNP)	4830	36·9%
Taylor Douglas (Conservative)	1250	9·5%
John Horne (LibDem)	849	6·4%
Joanne Telfer (SSP)	286	2·2%
Turnout: 60·3%		
Majority: 1074		

SOURCE 2 2005 UK General Election		
Candidate	Number of votes	Percentage of votes
Angus MacNeil (SNP)	6213	44·9%
Calum MacDonald (Labour)	4772	34·5%
Jean Davis (LibDem)	1096	7·9%
James Hargreaves (Other)	1048	7·6%
Andy Maciver (Conservative)	610	4·4%
Joanne Telfer (SSP)	97	0·7%
Turnout: 64·1%		
Majority: 1441		

Sources 1 and 2 show the results of the UK General Election in the Western Isles (Na h-Eileanan an Iar) Constituency in 2001 and 2005.

Study the two sources and write down *differences* between the 2001 result and the 2005 result.

Mention *two* differences in your answer.

Your answer must be based entirely on Sources 1 and 2 above. (4 marks)

A lot of information about the two election results is given in Sources 1 and 2. As in the previous question, some of the information is the same in both sources. For example, Joanne Telfer was the candidate for the SSP in both elections and came last in both elections. There are also many differences between the two election results. You should find two of the main differences and give evidence from the sources to back up your answer.

This is a weak answer.

In 2001 Calum MacDonald won, in 2005 he didn't.

This is a better answer.

The first difference between the election results in the Western Isles in 2001 and in 2005 is that in 2001, Calum MacDonald, the Labour candidate, won the election. <u>However</u>, in 2005 he came second, and Angus MacNeil, the SNP candidate, won because he had the most votes.

This is also a weak answer.

The turnout was different in the two elections.

Why is this a weak answer?

This gives no evidence to back up the point being made.

This is a better answer.

The second difference is that the turnout was different in the two elections. In 2001, turnout was only 60·3%, <u>but</u> in 2005 turnout had increased by about 4% to 64·1%.

Why is this a better answer?

This second version, giving a second difference, shows that you do not have to write a large amount in order to gain marks. This answer contains a number of good points:

- Information from both sources is given, which is essential if you are going to contrast and show differences.
- Figures are given from each of the sources as evidence.

- Evaluation is taking place by using evaluative words such as **'only'** and **'increased'**; this shows that the information has been understood and not just copied out.

- A rough calculation has been given of the difference in turnout – 'by about 4%'. It does not have to be exact to the decimal point.

In this final example, the front pages of two different newspapers from the same day are shown side by side. Both newspapers report the same story but have a different approach to how it is presented.

EXAM EXAMPLE 3

Front pages of *The Daily Express* and *The Guardian* on Thursday, 16 September 2004

Sources 1 and 2 show the front pages of two newspapers and how they reported the same story. One is a *tabloid*-style newspaper; the other is a *broadsheet*-style newspaper.

Study the two sources and write down *differences* between the ways the newspapers reported the same story.

Mention *two* differences in your answer.

Your answer must be based entirely on Sources 1 and 2 above.   (4 marks)

Once again, there are similarities between the two front pages. For example, both have the name of the newspaper at the top of the page, and both are reporting the same incident when a protest took place in the House of Commons. However, it is not the similarities you must write about, but the differences.

Three possible points of comparison which illustrate differences are numbered on the pictures.

The first difference is that, in Source 1, the Daily Express has only one large photograph and it takes up most of the page, while in Source 2, the Guardian, three photographs are used but they are smaller than in the Daily Express and do not take up as much of the page.

The second difference is in the headlines. In Source 1, the headline is shorter and tries to catch the reader's attention by using the phrase 'Tally Oh!' In the Guardian, Source 2, the headline is not written in such large type and is a more straightforward description of what the story is about. So, the Daily Express tries to attract your attention while the Guardian tries to give information.

During your Modern Studies course, you will almost certainly have studied newspapers and articles from newspapers to get information. You will probably also have discussed different types of newspapers, so the differences written about in the answer above should be familiar to you. However, all the information in the answer does not come from your own knowledge but by applying the skills you have learned to the two pictures.

In each case, the difference is noticed in the photographs, headline or articles, and evidence is given describing what the differences actually are. Evaluative words are used to point out the differences – **'only one'**, **'smaller'**, **'more straightforward'** and **'shorter'** are all used to contrast the way the two newspapers reported the story.

In all Evaluating questions, you must use all the sources given in order to get full marks. In this type of 'differences' question, you cannot answer without using the two sources – the whole point of the question is to look for and describe differences between two viewpoints, sets of figures or pictures. A comparison which shows differences must compare between at least two sources of information.

1   Using the question on the election result (question 2(e)), write down a difference about how well the Conservative Party did in the two elections.

2   Using the question on the newspaper front pages, in your own words write down the third ⬚3⬚ difference.

SUPPORT AND OPPOSE A POINT OF VIEW

This type of question may have one or two sources. In this type of question, after the source or sources, a viewpoint will be given. You may be asked to find pieces of evidence from the source or sources where:

●   both support (agree with) the view
●   both oppose (disagree with) the view
●   one supports and one opposes the view.

It is essential in this type of question, if there are two sources, that you use both sources of information. If this is the case, one piece of evidence must come from Source 1 and one must come from Source 2. You will not gain full marks if you take two pieces of evidence from the same source, even if both are correct. You must also refer to the viewpoint in your answer. This is the best way to answer the question, since it helps make sure that you are answering the question correctly and keeps you on the right lines. In some questions, the view may be in two parts, and it is essential to say which evidence agrees with which part of the view. In the case of those questions which ask you to find evidence to support and oppose a point of view, you must indicate clearly, by mentioning the view in your answer, which evidence supports and which evidence opposes the view.

The following examples from SQA past papers will illustrate how to answer this type of question.

EXAM EXAMPLE 4

Intermediate 1, 2007 paper, question 3(c)

Question 3 (continued)

(*c*) Study Sources 1 and 2 below, then answer the question which follows.

SOURCE 1

Poverty in Britain

Child poverty is still a big problem in Britain. In recent years the government has introduced a number of policies to try and tackle child poverty. The percentage of children living in households with less than half the average income fell from 18% to 11% between 2000 and 2004. The government has said it is determined to tackle child poverty in Britain.

SOURCE 2

Children living in families receiving benefits in the UK

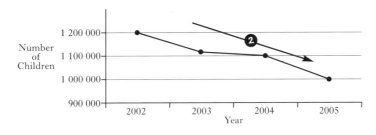

View of Peter Lees

Using the information in Sources 1 and 2 above, give **two** pieces of evidence to **oppose** the view of Peter Lees.

Your answer must be based entirely on Sources 1 and 2 above.

(4 marks)

This question contains two sources. So, in order to achieve full marks, both sources must be used in your answer.

The view of Peter Lees is in two parts:

- There has been no fall in child poverty levels ... in recent years.
- There has been no fall ... in the number of children living in families receiving benefits in recent years.

You are asked to find two pieces of evidence which oppose Peter Lees's view. There is evidence in Source 1 which opposes the first part of the view, and Source 2 contains evidence which opposes the second part of the view. To get full marks for this question, you must link the correct evidence with the correct part of the view. You must give enough evidence to back up the point you are making.

This is a good answer.

The first piece of evidence to oppose Peter Lees, when he says 'There has been no fall in child poverty levels in recent years', is in Source 1. Source 1 shows that the percentage of children living in households with less than half the average income fell from 18% to 11% between 2000 and 2004, so there has been a fall in child poverty levels.

Source 2 shows that the number of children living in families receiving benefits fell from 1 200 000 in 2002 to 1 million in 2005. This opposes Peter Lees's view when he says 'there has been no fall in the number of children living in families receiving benefits in recent years'.

Why is this a good answer?

The first part of the answer above begins with the first part of the view of Peter Lees and then links the view with the correct evidence from Source 1. The answer quotes the correct sentence with the evidence that opposes Peter Lees's view and mentions that it comes from Source 1.

The second part of the answer finds the evidence from Source 2 first. It accurately quotes the figures from the line graph. It uses the title of the line graph to explain the meaning of the figures, then quotes figures from 2002, showing that they have fallen in 2005. Another approach to using the figures could have been to say:

The number of children living in families receiving benefits in the UK fell by 200,000 from 2002 to 1 million in 2005.

After giving the evidence, the answer goes on to link it with the correct part of the view that it opposes.

EXAM EXAMPLE 5

Intermediate 1, 2006 paper, question 1(d)

Study the information below, then answer the question which follows.

Title

Age and Gender of Scottish Local Authority Councillors

		Councillors (%)
Age	21–29	2%
	30–44	20%
	45–59	51%
	Over 60	28%
Gender	Female	22%
	Male	78%

Figures in percentages

Women are just as likely to be councillors as men. Most councillors are between the ages of 45 and 59.

View of Jim White

Using the information above, give *one* piece of evidence to *support* the view of Jim White and one piece of evidence to *oppose* the view of Jim White.

Your answer must be based entirely on the information above.   (4 marks)

The question above has only one source, but it contains information about both the age and the gender of councillors. When using tables, the first thing you should do is make sure you carefully read the title of the table. This tells you what the information in the table is about: **Age and Gender of Scottish Local Authority Councillors**.

In this question, the view of Jim White is in two parts, in two separate sentences. You must refer to both parts of the view in your answer and accurately give the correct evidence to both support and oppose the view.

This is a good answer.

Jim White says that 'Women are just as likely to be councillors as men'. The evidence in the table <u>opposes</u> this view, as it shows that men are more likely to be councillors than women. The evidence is that 78% of councillors are men but only 22% of councillors are women.

Jim White also says that 'Most councillors are between the ages of 45 and 59'. The evidence in the table supports this part of his view, as the evidence shows that 51% of councillors are aged between 45 and 59 and this is just over half, while the next biggest age group is over-60s and that is only 28%.

Why is this is a good answer?

If you look carefully at the answer above, you will see that it uses our system of PEE. This time, the final E stands for **Evidence**:

It makes the point (P): 'Women are just as likely to be councillors as men'. The evidence in the table opposes this view ...

It explains the point (E): ... as it shows that men are more likely to be councillors than women ...

And finally, it gives evidence (E) to back up the explanation: ... The evidence is that 78% of councillors are men but only 22% of councillors are women.

The final example of this type of question has two sources and asks you to give two reasons to support the view. Both the sources are statistical, one in the form of a table and the other in the form of a bar chart. Careful and accurate use of statistical sources is an important skill to develop.

As mentioned earlier, the first thing to do with a statistical source is read the title of the table or graph. You should also look carefully at how the figures are presented, whether the information is presented as a number, as a percentage or a rate per hundred or per million, and so on.

In the following question, there is a single view given, and you must give a reason from each source to support the view of Cyril Mathee.

EXAM EXAMPLE 6

Intermediate 1, 2005 paper, question 9(c)

Question 9 (continued)

(c) Study Sources 1 and 2 below, then answer the question which follows.

SOURCE 1

Title ──────── **Number of murders with firearms in 2000 (Selected countries)**

Country	Numbers
South Africa	31 918
Colombia	21 898
Thailand	20 032
United States	8259
Mexico	3589
Zimbabwe	598
Germany	384

Figures given as numbers

SOURCE 2

Title ──────── **Murder rate per 100 000 of the population**

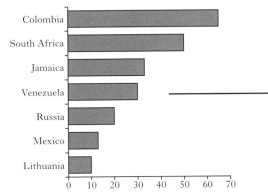

Figures given as a rate per 100 000.
• **Do not** say South Africa had 50 murders while Venezuela had 30 murders.
• **Do** say South Africa's murder rate was 50 per 100 000 people.

South Africa is one of the most dangerous countries of the world to live in.

View of Cyril Mathee

Using Sources 1 and 2 above, give **two** reasons to **support** the view of Cyril Mathee.

Your answer must be based entirely on Sources 1 and 2 above.

(4 marks)

This is a good answer.

South Africa is one of the most dangerous countries in the world to live in because, out of the selected countries in Source 1, it has the highest number of murders using firearms. The evidence is that it had 31 918 murders with firearms in 2000 while the next worst country, Colombia, had about 10 000 fewer, with 21 898.

The second reason to support the view of Cyril Mathee, that South Africa is one of the most dangerous countries in the world, is that it has a very high murder rate. The evidence is that, in Source 2, South Africa has the second highest rate of murder at 50 people murdered out of every 100 000 people; this is higher than Russia, which has a lower murder rate of 20 per 100 000 people.

DECISION-MAKING

This type of question appears in the Social Issues section of the exam paper and in unit assessments for the Social Issues unit. You may be studying Wealth and Health in the United Kingdom or Crime and the Law in Society. In each case, you will be given information and you will be asked to make a decision which you must support with evidence from the source and the circumstances you are given information about.

You will always be given two choices. There is no 'right' choice; either option can be chosen. Answering the question successfully is about giving the right reasons for your choice.

EXAM EXAMPLE 7

Intermediate 1, 2006 paper, question 4(d)

> Carefully read the introduction to the question, which tells you what you have to do.

> You have two options. After looking at both options and considering the information about Mrs Parveet Singh, you choose which option would be better.

(d)   Study the information below, then answer the question which follows.

You work for a charity that advises elderly people and their families about health treatment. You have to decide whether or not Mrs Parveet Singh should have a knee replacement operation.

Option 1

Have knee replacement operation

- Knee replacement will improve mobility considerably.
- High success rate for women.
- Will allow Parveet to remain at home.
- Long-term use of painkillers can cause health problems.

Option 2

Do not have knee replacement operation

- Being overweight can affect success rate of operation.
- There is a higher risk of infection if you have other health problems.
- Any surgery is risky, especially on people over 80.
- May eventually need to move into a nursing home.

Information about Mrs Parveet Singh

- Parveet has lived in Glasgow for forty years and is well known in the local community.
- Parveet is overweight.
- The Hindu centre for worship is close by, and she attends when she can.
- She has recently been in a lot of pain from arthritis in her knee.
- She is 82 years old.
- Her 85-year-old husband lives at home, and she cares for him.
- She has recently been told she has a heart condition.

Using the information above, **you must decide whether Mrs Parveet Singh should have a knee replacement operation (Option 1) or whether Mrs Parveet Singh should not have a knee replacement operation (Option 2).** Give **two** reasons to support your choice.

In your answer, **you must link the option you choose to the information about Mrs Parveet Singh**.

Answers to this type of question must link the information about Mrs Parveet Singh to the information in the option chosen. You would get no marks if you wrote the following weak answer.

I choose Option 1 as being best for Mrs Parveet Singh because having a knee replacement operation will improve her mobility and the second reason is that this operation has a high success rate for women.

Why is this a weak answer?

This gets no marks because there has been no use of the information about Mrs Singh. Both points are taken from Option 1 – they must be linked to Mrs Singh's circumstances in order to get any marks.

You can answer the question by choosing either Option 1 or Option 2. You should say at the start of your answer which option you are choosing.

This is a good answer.

I choose Option 1: Mrs Parveet Singh should have the knee replacement operation.

❶ *The first reason why Mrs Singh should have the operation is because Mrs Singh likes to attend the Hindu centre for worship when she can. The knee operation will improve her mobility so she will be able to get out more and attend the Hindu centre.*

❷ *The second reason why Mrs Singh should have the operation is because having the operation will allow her to remain at home. Mrs Singh would probably want to stay at home because her husband is 85 and she cares for him at home, so if she was not at home there would be no one to care for him.*

You could also have chosen Option 2.

This is a good answer.

I think Option 2 would be best for Mrs Singh because I think she should not have the knee replacement operation.

❸ *Being overweight can affect the success of the operation, and the information about Mrs Singh tells us that she is overweight, so the operation may not work.*

❹ *The second reason why I chose Option 2 is that Mrs Singh has recently been told that she has a heart condition, and in Option 2 it says that there is a higher risk of infection if you have other health problems, so this would mean a higher risk for Mrs Singh.*

In this type of question, there are many different answers, but you must make sure that you explain why the option you have chosen is best for the circumstances. To do this, you have to link information from the option chosen and the circumstances of the person.

CONCLUSIONS

In this type of question, you will be given information in one or two sources. You must use this information to give conclusions. This means explaining which are the important or significant things you can see in the information. It is no use just writing out the information again. You must judge what is important and use the evidence to back up your judgement or conclusion.

Conclusions can be judgements about:

- The biggest
- The smallest
- Changes over time
- Something has got better
- Something has got worse
- Differences

The following two examples show how you can give conclusions.

The first example is from the 2007 exam paper and gives information about unemployment rates for different racial groups in the United States of America.

EXAM EXAMPLE 8

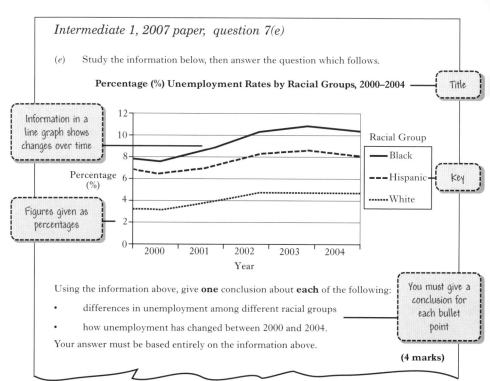

Intermediate 1, 2007 paper, question 7(e)

(e) Study the information below, then answer the question which follows.

Percentage (%) Unemployment Rates by Racial Groups, 2000–2004 —— Title

Information in a line graph shows changes over time

Percentage (%)

Figures given as percentages

Racial Group

—— Black
--- Hispanic ── Key
······ White

Year

Using the information above, give **one** conclusion about **each** of the following:

- differences in unemployment among different racial groups
- how unemployment has changed between 2000 and 2004.

Your answer must be based entirely on the information above.

You must give a conclusion for each bullet point

(4 marks)

You are asked to give a conclusion about:

● differences in unemployment among different racial groups.

From the information in the line graph, you can see that, between 2000 and 2004, unemployment rates are given for Blacks, Hispanics and Whites. By using the key, you can also see that the Black level of unemployment is always the highest and the White unemployment rate is always the lowest. The Hispanic rate is between that of Blacks and Whites.

You would be likely to decide that the most important thing the information tells us about the 'differences in unemployment among different racial groups' is that Blacks always have the highest level and Whites always have the lowest level.

You would provide evidence for this conclusion by giving figures, as evidence, from the line graph to back up your conclusion.

This is a good answer.

The first conclusion is about differences in unemployment among different racial groups. The evidence shows that the rate of unemployment for Blacks in the USA is always higher than for Hispanics and for Whites, and that, out of the three groups, Whites always have the lowest rate of unemployment. The evidence for this is that the Black unemployment rate in 2000 was about 8% and in 2004 it was just above 10%, while the unemployment rate for Whites in 2000 was just over 3% and it was about 4·5% in 2004.

You are also asked to draw a conclusion about:

- how unemployment has changed between 2000 and 2004.

In this conclusion, you are looking for any trend over the five years shown in the graph. For each racial group, the unemployment level is higher in 2004 than it was in 2000.

This is a good answer.

Unemployment for all three racial groups shown in the graph has increased between 2000 and 2004. For Blacks, the rate of unemployment rose from about 8% to about 10%, for Hispanics it also went up from 7% to 8%, and it went up for Whites from about 3% to about 4·5% in 2004.

EXAM EXAMPLE 9

Intermediate 1, 2006 paper, question 2(c)

(c)   Study Sources 1 and 2 below, then answer the question which follows.

SOURCE 1

Scottish Parliament: Women and Ethnic Minority MSPs in 2003

Group	Number of MSPs	Percentage (%) of MSPs
Women	51	40%
Ethnic minorities	0	0%

SOURCE 2

UK Parliament: Women and Ethnic Minority MPs in 2001

Group	Number of MPs	Percentage (%) of MPs
Women	118	18%
Ethnic minorities	12	2%

Using the information in Sources 1 and 2 above, what **conclusion** can you reach about each of the following:

- women in the Scottish and UK Parliaments
- ethnic minorities in the Scottish and UK Parliaments?

Your answer must be based entirely on Sources 1 and 2 above.

(4 marks)

In the above example, you are using information from two sources; one table gives information about the Scottish Parliament, the other about the UK Parliament.

You are asked to draw conclusions by comparing the information. Be careful that you do not just copy out the information without coming to a conclusion. For example:

This is a weak answer.

There are 51 women in the Scottish Parliament; this is 40% of the MSPs. In the UK Parliament, there are 118 women. This is 18% of the MPs.

Why is this a weak answer?

All that this answer has done is rewrite the information in the two tables; no conclusion has been given, so no marks would be given.

Your conclusion can come at the start of your answer and you then give the evidence to support your conclusion, or it can come at the end, following the evidence. If we use the answer above, which up to now has no marks, we can turn it into a better one by adding a conclusion at the end.

This is a good answer.

There are 51 women in the Scottish Parliament; this is 40% of the MSPs. In the UK Parliament, there are 118 women. This is 18% of the MPs. My conclusion is that women are better represented in the Scottish Parliament than in the UK Parliament because they make up a much higher percentage of the members in the Scottish Parliament.

My conclusion about ethnic minorities is that ethnic minorities are better represented in the UK Parliament than in the Scottish Parliament. The evidence for this conclusion is that there were no ethnic minority MSPs while in the UK Parliament there were 12 ethnic minority MPs which is 2% of the total.

In the first paragraph, the conclusion comes at the end after the evidence has been given. The second paragraph begins with the conclusion and then uses evidence from both the sources to back up the conclusion. Either approach is acceptable; as long as your answer has a conclusion, it does not matter where it appears.

Do not just copy out information from the sources. You must draw conclusions by making a judgement about what is important in the information.

EXAGGERATION

In this type of question, you will be given factual information in one or two sources followed by a view:

> Most of the money spent by the Common Agricultural Policy goes on helping farmers get a good price for their crops. Helping rural development is the second largest item of spending. 75% of EU farmers have to survive on less than €7000 per year. Small farms get a big percentage of the money paid to farmers.

View of EU spokesperson

The view will contain four sentences. By comparing the information in the sources with the view, you should see that two of the sentences are accurate and based upon the facts. However, two of the sentences in the view are not factually based and are exaggerated. Exaggerated statements will be ones that are not accurate and not based upon the facts. They may make something out to be worse than it really is or better than it is in fact.

In this question, you must identify and write down each sentence that is exaggerated and give evidence from the sources to show why it is exaggerated.

EXAM EXAMPLE 10

Intermediate 1, 2005 paper, question 6(c)

(c)   Study Sources 1 and 2 below, then answer the question which follows.

SOURCE 1

Factfile – The Common Agricultural Policy (CAP) ······ Factfile

- The CAP costs €40 billion per year
- Spending on agriculture is half the €80 billion budget of the European Union
- A family of four spends €12 more on food in a week than it should because the CAP keeps prices high
- 75% of EU farmers have to survive on less than €7000 per year
- Small farms make up 40% of EU farms but get only 8% of the money paid to farms
- Five large farms in the UK each get more than €1 million per year in help from the EU

€ = Euro

SOURCE 2
What Common Agricultural Fund money is spent on ——— Title

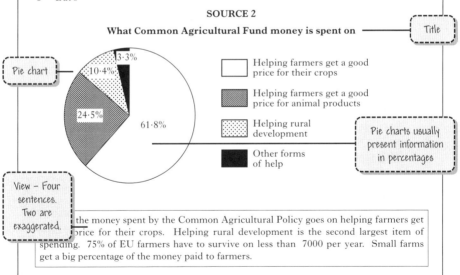

Pie chart

3·3%
10·4%
24·5%
61·8%

☐ Helping farmers get a good price for their crops

▨ Helping farmers get a good price for animal products

▦ Helping rural development

■ Other forms of help

Pie charts usually present information in percentages

View – Four sentences. Two are exaggerated.

the money spent by the Common Agricultural Policy goes on helping farmers get price for their crops. Helping rural development is the second largest item of spending. 75% of EU farmers have to survive on less than 7000 per year. Small farms get a big percentage of the money paid to farmers.

View of EU spokesperson

Write down **two** examples of **exaggeration** from the statement by the EU spokesperson.

For each example, give **one** reason why it is exaggerated.

Your answer must be based entirely on Sources 1 and 2 above.

(4 marks)

Let's look at the four sentences in the view of the EU spokesperson:

Sentence	Exaggerated?
Most of the money spent by the Common Agricultural Policy goes on helping farmers get a good price for their crops.	**No** – Source 2 shows this is correct
Helping rural development is the second largest item of spending.	**Yes** – Source 2 shows this is exaggerated
75% of EU farmers have to survive on less than €7000 per year.	**No** – Source 1 shows this is correct
Small farms get a big percentage of the money paid to farmers.	**Yes** – Source 1 shows this is exaggerated

The table above shows which of the four sentences in the view are exaggerated.

This is a good answer.

The first example of exaggeration is when the EU spokesperson says 'Helping rural development is the second largest item of spending'. This is exaggerated because Source 2 shows me that helping rural development is the third biggest item of spending at only 10·4%. Both 'Helping farmers get a good price for their crops' and 'Helping farmers get a good price for animal products' have a higher percentage spent on them than rural development.

The second sentence that is exaggerated is when the EU spokesperson says 'Small farms get a big percentage of the money paid to farmers'. This is exaggerated because the Factfile in Source 1 shows that small farmers only get 8% of the money paid to farms when they make up 40% of the EU farms.

Why is this a good answer?

The best way to answer this type of question is to study the information in the sources and find the two sentences which are exaggerated. Answer the question by quoting the first sentence that is exaggerated, then follow this with the evidence which proves it is exaggerated. Then give the second sentence which is exaggerated and give the evidence from the source which proves it is exaggerated.

If there are two sources, you will have to use both, so the evidence for one example of exaggeration will come from one source while the evidence for the other example of exaggeration will come from the other source.

Answering Evaluating Questions at Intermediate 2

Support and oppose a point of view

The Decision-Making Task

Selective use of facts

Conclusions

At Intermediate 2 level, Evaluating questions are source-based questions where you are able to show your skills in using the information in the sources to:

- support or oppose a point of view
- make decisions
- explain selectivity in the use of facts
- draw conclusions.

These questions are generally worth **8 marks**, although the Decision-Making Task in Section B – Social Issues in the United Kingdom – is worth **10 marks**.

Questions usually consist of three sources, which may be written, written in the form of a factfile, and statistical in the form of tables, graphs or charts. In order to gain full marks, you must use all the sources in your answer. Good-quality answers will link information across the sources and gain high marks.

SUPPORT AND OPPOSE A POINT OF VIEW

In this type of question, a viewpoint is given, and you must use the evidence to give two reasons to support and two reasons to oppose the viewpoint. It is essential that you refer clearly to the viewpoint in your answer. It is sometimes not possible to give any marks if the answer immediately begins by using information from the sources without saying clearly whether the evidence is supporting or opposing the view. It is important that your answer has a logical structure.

EXAM EXAMPLE 1

Intermediate 2, 2007 paper, question 1(c)

SOURCE 1

Make Poverty History Campaign

The Make Poverty History Campaign organised a demonstration to put pressure on the leaders of the eight richest countries in the world, known as G8. The demonstration, which took place in July 2005 in Edinburgh, was one of the largest ever in Scotland. It aimed to influence the G8 leaders meeting in nearby Gleneagles.

The leaders would be meeting to consider aid, trade and debt relief for the poorest nations in the world. Almost a quarter of a million people from all walks of life and from all over the UK came to Edinburgh to tell the G8 leaders that real action must be taken to reduce poverty around the world. First Minister, Jack McConnell, and Chancellor of the Exchequer, Gordon Brown, both attended the demonstration and expressed their support for the campaign.

The demonstration was made up of young, middle-aged and older people, members of trade unions, church groups and anti-poverty organisations. On a sunny day, the thousands attending listened to speeches and music and marched around Edinburgh getting their message across to the newspapers and television broadcasters who covered the event.

It was a pity that many of the reports the next day focused upon the small group of radical protesters who threatened to break away from the official demonstration and cause violence and damage.

SOURCE 2

Direct Action at G8 Summit

As the leaders of the G8 countries met behind a ring of steel at Gleneagles Hotel, violence erupted outside. Dozens of protesters disrupted traffic across Scotland by sitting down in the middle of motorways and blocking railway lines. A few attacked buildings and cars in nearby Stirling, leading to violent confrontations with the police.

Later that day, as the protest march at Gleneagles came to an end, a few hundred protesters tried to break down the steel fence surrounding the hotel. Hundreds of police were moved into the area to stop the demonstrators breaking through. Police using riot shields, batons and dogs kept the protesters out, and there were casualties on both sides.

The violent protests gained a lot of publicity in the media. Make Poverty History campaigners criticised the violence and claimed it had nothing to do with the message they were trying to get across. First Minister, Jack McConnell, said the violence and property damage would not help the poorest countries in Africa.

Groups such as Dissent, the Wombles and the Clandestine Insurgent Rebel Clown Army felt they were successful in forcing the leaders of rich countries to listen. They urged the public to continue other forms of direct action such as boycotting products to put pressure on the rich countries.

Question 1 (c) (continued)

SOURCE 3

Result of Survey on Involvement in Forms of Political Action

Level of participation in activity	Survey Question: Over the past twelve months, have you taken part in any of the following actions to influence rules, laws or policies?	
	Form of Action	Percentage answering yes
Less active participation	Donated money to an organisation	67%
	Signed a petition	50%
	Bought certain products as part of a campaign	39%
	Raised funds for an organisation	32%
	Worn or displayed a campaign badge or sticker	28%
	Attended a political meeting or rally	7%
	Taken part in a public demonstration	6%
	Boycotted certain products	41%
	Contacted the media	11%
More active participation	Participated in illegal protest activities	2%

> Pressure groups can only achieve their aims if they use direct action and illegal methods.
>
> View of Bob Ure

Using Sources 1, 2 and 3 above and opposite, give **two** reasons to **support** and **two** reasons to **oppose** the view of Bob Ure.

Your answer must be based entirely on the Sources.

You must use information from each Source in your answer.

(8 marks)

This is a good start.

The first reason to support the view of Bob Ure when he says 'pressure groups can only achieve their aims if they use direct action and illegal methods' is ...

Why is this a good start?

This opening sentence, in our first example, is a good start since it refers to the view and clearly indicates that the first reason given in the answer will be to support the view. You must make full use of the sources in your answer; in order to score high marks, it is not enough to take one point from any source without linking it to another point or explaining its importance or relevance.

... Source 2 says that dozens of protesters disrupted traffic across Scotland and blocked railway lines and also says a few hundred protesters tried to break down the steel fencing surrounding the hotel at Gleneagles. These actions gained a lot of publicity in the media, so they did achieve their aims of being noticed.

The point above links together several separate points from Source 2 to give a detailed reason to support the view. While it uses words from the source, it does not just copy out sentences exactly as they appear in the source. The final point also comes from the source and gives an explanation of the information that has already been given and how it is linked to the view.

Good answers will bring together information from different parts of one source and between different sources. This means linking information from different sources to give added weight to the reasons being given or making comparisons. You will not gain marks by copying out large chunks of information from the sources without any explanation.

The first point can be improved by giving information from Source 1 which makes the explanation stronger.

Source 1 also states that, in spite of a very large, peaceful demonstration being held in Edinburgh, many of the reports the next day focused upon the small group of protesters who threatened to break away from the official demonstration and cause violence and damage.

Being able to link information from more than one source is the sign of a very high-quality answer and is a demonstration of sophisticated Modern Studies skills in using information and giving evidence.

When using statistics, it is important to use the statistical information accurately and quote the figures given in the source to support the answer. Since statistics can often be used to both support and oppose a point of view, it is important to explain the relevance of the statistics and how they support the reasons being given.

This is a good point.

A reason to <u>oppose</u> the view of Bob Ure who states that 'pressure groups can only achieve their aims if they use direct action and illegal methods' is that Source 3 shows that a large percentage of people are prepared to take part in legal and peaceful forms of action; for example, 67%, the highest figure in the table, have donated money to an organisation in the last twelve months and 50% have signed a petition. Only a small percentage (2%) participated in illegal protest activities, so pressure groups do not have to use illegal methods to attract a lot of support.

As mentioned earlier, high-quality answers will synthesise information across the sources. Statistics from one source can often be used to back up evidence given from written sources. You should look for these links between sources to give in your answer.

This is a very good point.

A second reason to <u>support</u> the view of Bob Ure when he says pressure groups can only achieve their aims when they use direct action is shown in Source 2 and Source 3. Source 2 says that groups such as Dissent and the Wombles felt they were successful in forcing the leaders of rich countries to listen and urged the public to continue forms of direct action such as boycotting products to put pressure on rich countries. Source 3 shows us that 41% of the public had boycotted certain products in the last twelve months, which is one of the highest figures in the forms of action taken.

In the second example which follows, three sources are included which give information about crime and treatment of criminals in China. The sources are in the form of a factfile, a statistical table and a written source. Evidence from all sources must be included in your answer if you are to get full marks. No matter how good your answer, if you only use two sources you can only score a maximum of 6 marks, and if you only use one source you can only gain a maximum of 4 marks.

You must explain how the evidence you have used from the sources either supports or opposes the view given. You may think it is obvious when you are writing the answer, but the person marking the answer must be sure that you understand what you are doing and what the evidence means.

In this question, the view which you must give reasons to support and oppose is:

China is harsh and effective in its treatment of criminals.

View of a Chinese crime researcher

EXAM EXAMPLE 2

Intermediate 2, 2006 paper, question 8(c)

(c)   Study Sources 1, 2 and 3 below and opposite, then answer the question which follows.

SOURCE 1

Factfile – Crime in China

- In China, many crimes are punished by death including bribery, drug dealing, stealing petrol and violent crime.

- China is only fourteenth in the world for the number of executions per million people.

- In the first three months of 2004, there were 923 000 criminal cases reported in China, a 14·2% increase over the same period in 2003.

- Police were successful in clearing up 285 000 cases in the first three months of 2004. This was 1·6% higher than at the start of 2003.

- There were 639 theft cases in the first three months of 2004: an increase of 17·1% over the same time in 2003.

- Following the murder of four students in Guangxi province, police tracked down the criminal and arrested him within three weeks.

- One man was accused of 65 cases of murder in 2003. Police were criticised for keeping the case secret instead of asking the public for help.

Continued on next page

Question 8 (c) (continued)

SOURCE 2

Number of Executions in Selected Countries, 2002

Country	Number of executions	Number of executions per million people
China	1067	0·82 per million
Democratic Republic of Congo	100	1·76 per million
United States	68	0·23 per million
Iran	66	0·96 per million
Egypt	48	0·64 per million
Belarus	33	3·19 per million
Taiwan	32	1·41 per million

SOURCE 3

Dealing with Drug Addiction in Yunnan Province

South-West China's Yunnan province has China's biggest drug problem. The authorities argue that the province's 41 million people are innocent victims of the international trade in heroin. Four-fifths of China's opium seizures are in Yunnan province. Along the drug supply routes, cases of drug addiction and HIV/AIDS have increased.

In Yunnan, a mixture of tactics is used to fight the drug problem. Tough tactics are used against drug dealers. About 400 drug dealers are executed each year in the province. Also in Yunnan, an unusual experiment has taken place. Rehabilitation centres have been set up with the emphasis on prevention and cure. In contrast, police in the rest of China treat addicts as criminals. Addicts picked up for the first time in Yunnan are sent for three months' detoxification in special centres. This involves using herbal pills, counselling and the discipline of an army camp. The police in Yunnan say that there is a need for community care and counselling when addicts return home. They also call for education programmes at school. Centres in Yunnan have a caring approach which has had considerable success in keeping people off drugs.

China is harsh and effective in its treatment of criminals.

View of a Chinese crime researcher

Using Sources 1, 2 and 3 above and opposite, give **two** reasons to **support** and **two** reasons to **oppose** the view of the Chinese crime researcher.

Your answer must be based entirely on the Sources above and opposite.

(8 marks)

You must explain why the evidence you have used either supports or opposes the point of view. Do not leave the evidence to 'speak for itself'. It may seem obvious to you, but you must show the marker that you understand the evidence.

The answers which score the highest marks are the ones which synthesise information from across the sources. This means that you link evidence from different sources to make a stronger point.

Sometimes, answers to this type of question begin by giving a piece of evidence almost exactly from the source without making any reference to the view.

This is weak use of evidence.

In China, many crimes are punished by the death penalty such as bribery, drug dealing and stealing petrol. **1**

Why is this weak use of evidence?

Clearly, this is taken almost without change from the first point in the factfile (Source 1). However, there is no explanation of how this relates to the viewpoint or whether it is supporting the view or opposing the view. On its own, it cannot be given any marks, although the person writing the answer may believe it is obvious that the point is meant to support the view, since it shows China being harsh: it gives the death penalty for crimes which, although serious, would generally not suffer the death penalty in other countries. This has not been said in the answer.

To begin this type of answer correctly, you must show whether the evidence you are giving supports or opposes the view. A **simple structure** will make sure you do this.

This is a better point.

The first reason to <u>support</u> the view that China is harsh and effective in its treatment of criminals is that, in China, many crimes are punished by the death penalty such as bribery, drug dealing and stealing petrol. This shows that China is very harsh in the way it treats some criminals.

Why is this a better point?

This is a basic point, but it does make sure that the marker knows that the evidence is being used to support the view and shows understanding of the evidence being used by giving a brief explanation at the end.

There is also evidence in Source 1 which opposes the view – so, when you turn to this part of the question, you must show that you are now giving evidence which does not support the view. You should begin this part of the answer in a new paragraph:

This is a good point.

The first reason to <u>oppose</u> the view of the Chinese crime researcher when he says that China is harsh and effective in its treatment of criminals is that crime has been rising in China. Source 1 shows that, in the first three months of 2004, there were 923 000 criminal cases reported in China, which was an increase of 14·2% compared with 2003. Source 1 also shows that there had been an increase in theft cases of 17·1% between the first three months of 2003 and 2004. This evidence shows that China has not been effective in its treatment of criminals, since crime is getting worse. 2

Why is this is a good point?

This part of the answer starts well by saying that the evidence opposes the view. It also gives some explanation at the end of why it opposes the view – 'not been effective in its treatment of criminals, since crime is getting worse'. The answer is better than the first example, since it takes two points from the same source and links them together to make a stronger argument. This would be given more marks, since more evidence is being given and it is being combined.

While linking related information from within the same source shows good practice, the best answers will link information together from different sources:

This shows good linking of evidence from different sources.

The second reason to <u>support</u> the view that China is harsh in its treatment of criminals is because it uses the death penalty for many crimes. Although Source 1 says that China is only fourteenth in the world for the number of executions per million people, Source 2 shows that the number of executions in China in 2002 was 1067; this is by far the largest number of the countries shown, with the next largest country only having 100 executions. This shows that China is the harshest in its treatment of criminals with the death penalty. 3

Source 3 must also be used to give evidence and gain full marks.

This is good explanation of evidence.

A reason to <u>support</u> the view that China is harsh and effective in its treatment of criminals is that Source 3 shows that tough tactics are used against drug dealers and that in Yunnan province about 400 drug dealers are executed each year; this shows that they are harsh in their punishment. Source 3 also shows that they are effective because in Yunnan they have set up rehabilitation centres which try to prevent and cure drug addicts, who are sent to detoxification centres for three months. This shows that China is harsh and effective because they use a mixture of tactics to fight the drug problem. **4**

THE DECISION-MAKING TASK

This type of question is always part of Section B in the exam – Social Issues in the United Kingdom – and is worth **10 marks**. You are asked to use the evidence to support the choice of a particular policy option. Evidence in the sources will be a mixture of written information, usually in the form of a factfile or contrasting viewpoints, and statistical information. You must also, for full marks, say why you did not choose the other option.

A lot of information will be given in the sources, as the questions are designed to contain enough evidence to allow you to choose either of the options given. It is very likely that you will have knowledge and understanding of the topic in the question, since you will have studied this topic in depth in class. However, this exercise is one which involves the use of the evidence in the sources to support a decision. Your own knowledge and understanding will help you in putting the information into context; however, no extra marks will be given if you include your own background knowledge in the answer.

This type of question at Intermediate 2 is slightly different from the Decision-Making Exercise at Higher and may cause confusion for students who have moved from a Higher class or are being taught in classes with Higher students. You will not lose any marks if you include your own knowledge, but you may use less of the information in the sources and also use up valuable time.

Using a report style is a good way to organise and present the large amount of information available in this type of question (as is the case with the Higher Decision-Making Exercise). It should be noted, however, that all aspects of the Higher DME are not the same as in the Decision-Making Task at Intermediate level. To answer this question well, you should give a recommendation at the start of your answer. You should give reasons to support your choice of option. You are not required to give reasons to oppose the option you have chosen, as at Higher. If you do this, you will be using valuable time without gaining any extra marks. You do, however, have to explain why you did not make the other choice, and failure to do this will result in a maximum of 8 marks being awarded. This explanation does not have to come at the end of the answer, although it is clearer to markers if it is included as a brief section at the end of the report-style answer.

In summary:

- Give a clear recommendation of the option you choose at the start.
- Give reasons, using the evidence from the sources, to support your recommendation.
- You should give at least four developed points which link information within and between the sources.
- Say why you did not choose the other option.
- Write in a report style, with headings.
- Use all the sources in your answer.

 There is not a 'right' answer to this question. You can choose either option, and there should be enough evidence to support your choice.

EXAM EXAMPLE 3

Intermediate 2, 2007 paper, question 4(c)

(c) Study Sources 1, 2 and 3 below and opposite, then answer the question which follows.

You are an adviser to the UK Government. You have been asked to recommend whether or not the police should be given additional powers to detain terrorist suspects for up to 90 days without charge.

Option 1	Option 2
Give police additional powers to detain terrorist suspects for up to 90 days without charge.	Do not give police additional powers to detain terrorist suspects for up to 90 days without charge.

SOURCE 1

Selected Facts and Viewpoints

- Detention for 90 days is against civil liberties. ❹
- Since the attacks on the USA on 11 September 2001, Britain has also been a target for terrorists. ❶
- The increased threat from international terrorism means that the police need increased powers.
- To increase maximum detention to 90 days would be against the UK's international human-rights responsibilities ❷
- The complexity of a terrorist investigation means that police need more time to investigate before charges are brought.
- Imprisonment without charge for 90 days will do more harm than good and lead to resentment and more recruits to terrorism.
- Supporters argue that the police need the extra time because of the difficulties of gathering evidence from overseas and from coded computer messages.
- The rights of those detained would be protected because a judge would need to approve the continuing detention at regular intervals throughout the 90 days.
- The increased powers could lead to a worsening of community and race relations in the UK.

SOURCE 2
Arrests in the UK under the Terrorism Act 2000, September 2001 to September 2005

Convicted of offences under the Terrorism Act	23
Charged under the Terrorism Act	115
Charged under other legislation	156
Transferred to Immigration authorities	63
Released without charge	496
Other outcomes	42
Total arrests	**895**

❸

Continued on next page

Question 4 (c) (continued)

SOURCE 2 (continued)
Results of a YouGov Poll
Question
Do you think it may sometimes be necessary to restrict the civil liberties of suspected terrorists even though there is not enough evidence to charge and convict them?

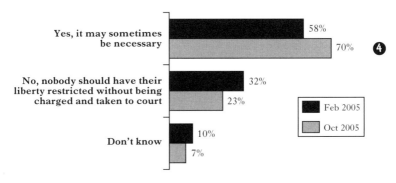

SOURCE 3

Viewpoints

The police should be given powers to detain terrorist suspects for up to 90 days due to the recent increase in the threat of terrorism. It would only be in a very few cases where a person would have to be detained for the full 90 days. More time is needed to gather evidence against suspects because of the nature of attacks like the 2005 London bombings. The investigations into the events of July 2005 produced 80 000 videos of CCTV footage and 1400 sets of fingerprints at 160 suspected crime scenes.

Police Spokesperson

The police should not be given powers to detain terrorist suspects for up to 90 days; the current 28-day rule is sufficient. It is just as bad as detention without trial. The Law Lords have ruled that detention without trial is illegal and unacceptable. It seriously undermines the right to a fair trial and the principle that you are innocent until proven guilty. This country is in danger of abandoning its democratic values.

Human Rights Spokesperson

You must decide which option to recommend to the UK Government, **either** to give the police additional powers **or** not to give the police additional powers to detain terrorist suspects for up to 90 days without charge.

Using Sources 1, 2 and 3 above and opposite, **which option would you choose**?

Give reasons to **support** your choice.

Explain why you did not make the other choice.

Your answer must be based on all the Sources.

(10 marks)

As is the case in other Evaluating questions, all sources must be used in the answer for full marks.

To answer this type of question successfully, you should state clearly which option you recommend. Use headings to show the different parts of this answer:

Recommendation

I am an adviser to the UK Government. I have been asked to recommend whether the police should be given additional powers to detain terrorist suspects for up to 90 days without charge. I choose Option 1 – the police should be given additional powers.

In a new section, with a heading, you should give reasons from the sources to support your choice:

This is a weak point.

Reasons to support Option 1 - Give the police additional powers

The first reason to give the police increased powers comes from Source 1 because it says that, since the attacks on the USA in 2001, Britain has become a target for terrorists. **1**

Why is this a weak point?

This is a simple and basic point without any development taken from bullet point 2 in Source 1, and, although it is accurate and correctly used, would not gain many marks on its own.

Your second point should start in a new paragraph.

This is a good point.

The second reason to support Option 1 is that Source 1 states that the complexity of a terrorist investigation means that police need more time to investigate before charges are brought. The Police Spokesperson in Source 3 agrees with this because he says that the investigations into the London bombings in July 2005 produced 80 000 videos of CCTV footage and 1400 sets of fingerprints at 160 suspected crime scenes, therefore 90 days may be necessary to study all of this evidence. **2**

This is a much better-developed point which links information from Source 1 and Source 3 and shows understanding of the evidence by giving an explanation. This point would score more marks than the previous, much more basic point.

Written information is usually more obviously linked to one or other of the options, although you should always explain the evidence you use. Statistical evidence may be less obvious and also requires explanation. If information is included, especially statistical information, and the importance and meaning of it is not explained, it may get no marks. In this question, Source 2 contains information about 'Arrests in the UK under the Terrorism Act 2000, September 2001 to September 2005'. The evidence could be used to support both options depending upon how the information is used:

> The information in Source 2 supports Option 1. Only 23 people were convicted under the Terrorism Act between September 2001 and September 2005 out of a total of 895 arrests. This is a very small proportion and shows that the police do need more powers to detain terrorist suspects for up to 90 days in order to get more convictions. $\boxed{3}$

Or

> The information in Source 2 supports Option 2. Only 23 people were convicted under the Terrorism Act between September 2001 and September 2005 out of a total of 895 arrests. This shows that it would be wrong to give the police the power to detain suspects for up to 90 days because a very large number of people would be detained for a long time without being convicted. $\boxed{3}$

Each of the points above uses the same information but draws different and valid conclusions. The explanation and interpretation of the statistics allows the figures from Source 2 to be used to support either option. On their own, without explanation, using the figures in your answer would not gain marks.

In order to gain full marks in the Decision-Making Task, you must also explain why you did not make the other choice. You should not repeat arguments already used in the reasons to support the option chosen. You will get no marks for saying something like 'I did not support the other option because there was no evidence to support it', as no evidence has actually been used. One approach would be to use new information not already used in your answer. Another way would be to recognise evidence which could be used to support the other option and use evidence to give a counter-argument:

> Reason for not recommending Option 2
>
> Although Source 1 says detention for 90 days is against civil liberties and would be against the UK's international human-rights responsibilities, the YouGov Poll shows that a majority of people think it may be necessary to restrict the civil liberties of suspected terrorists and that the percentage has increased from 58% to 70% between February 2005 and October 2005, therefore I do not choose Option 2. $\boxed{4}$

In the question which follows, taken from the 2006 SQA paper, the issue you are asked to make a recommendation about is one which you may have your own, strong opinions about. You must not let your own opinions get in the way of the evidence. You should be able to find evidence in the sources to support either of the options, but remember – this is an exercise in which you must use evidence to support a decision, not your own views.

EXAM EXAMPLE 4

Intermediate 2, 2006 paper, question 4(c)

(c)   Study Sources 1, 2 and 3 below and opposite, then answer the question which follows.

You are an adviser to the Scottish Executive. You have been asked to recommend whether or not to continue the ban on smoking in enclosed public places in order to improve health.

Option 1	**Option 2**
Continue the ban on smoking in enclosed public places.	Do not continue the ban on smoking in enclosed public places.

In this question, the statistical information comes at the beginning. The first part of Source 1 is in the form of a line graph. Line graphs are useful to show change over a period of time, in this case from 1974 to 2002. The key at the side also tells you that the three lines refer to percentage figures for smoking among men, women and the whole population. (Note that, although the smoking ban was introduced in 2006, the figures only go up to 2002 – these were the most up-to-date figures available at the time, since some statistics may take some time to be collected and published.)

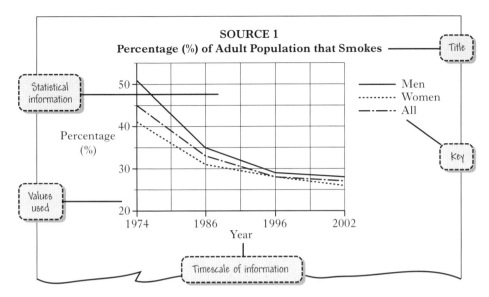

SOURCE 1
Percentage (%) of Adult Population that Smokes ——— Title

Statistical information

Men
Women
All

Percentage (%)

Key

Values used

50
40
30
20

1974   1986   1996   2002
Year

Timescale of information

Sometimes, statistical information can be used to support either of the options. In some cases, this is not the case and you should not try to distort the information to force it to support whatever option you have chosen. However, the information in the source above may be used to support either option:

The information in Source 1, which shows the percentage of the adult population which smokes, <u>supports Option 1</u>, that the ban on smoking in enclosed public places should continue. The figures show that in 2002 about 26% of women smoked and about 28% of men smoked. The ban should continue, since this would give those people who still smoke more encouragement to give up and stop smoking. It is also the case that, since only about 27% of adults smoke, the majority of 73% do not smoke and they should not have to breathe in the smoke in enclosed places from those who do smoke.

Or

The information in Source 1, which shows the percentage of the adult population which smokes, <u>supports Option 2</u>, that the ban on smoking in enclosed public places should not continue. The figures show that, between 1974 and 2002, the percentage of people smoking fell from 45% to 27%; for men it fell from over half smoking to about 28%, and for women it fell from just over 40% to 26%. This evidence shows that the percentage of people smoking is falling and therefore there is no need to continue the ban on smoking in public places, since most people are giving up smoking anyway and it is only a minority who still smoke.

Linking with information in other sources

Although each of the above points make good use of the statistics by stating clearly on which side of the argument the figures are being used, accurately quoting figures and, most importantly, explaining why the evidence used supports the chosen option, both points can be made even better by linking each with information from another source. In this case, Source 2, Selected Facts and Viewpoints (on page 88):

Option 1 is also supported by Source 2, which states that 'It has been found that a smoke-free environment encourages smokers to reduce the number of cigarettes smoked or to quit altogether', so banning smoking in enclosed places should lead to more people giving up, and more of the 27% of adults who still smoke would stop.

Or

Option 2 is also supported by Source 2, which states that 'In a survey, seven out of 10 people did not support a ban on smoking in pubs, restaurants and clubs'. So, even though a minority still smoke, a majority do not support the ban on smoking in public places.

(c) Study Sources 1, 2 and 3 below and opposite, then answer the question which follows.

You are an adviser to the Scottish Executive. You have been asked to recommend whether or not to continue the ban on smoking in enclosed public places in order to improve health.

Option 1	Option 2
Continue the ban on smoking in enclosed public places.	Do not continue the ban on smoking in enclosed public places.

SOURCE 1
Percentage (%) of Adult Population that Smokes

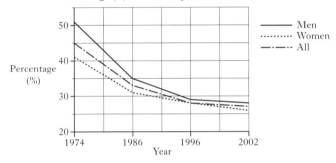

Results of a Health Survey of Parents with Children under 10 Years of Age

Does passive smoking result in the following health problems in children?	Percentage (%) saying 'Yes'
Asthma	26%
Lung infections	22%
Cancer	11%
Coughs/sore throat	5%
Bronchitis	5%

Number of Deaths from Selected Causes Linked to Smoking and Passive Smoking in Scotland per Year

Cause of Death	Total Deaths	Deaths linked to smoking	Deaths linked to passive smoking
Lung cancer	4000	3123	44
Heart disease	11 700	3767	395
Stroke	6750	1540	335
Respiratory	6500	2700	91
Total	**28 950**	**11 130**	**865**

Continued on next page

SOURCE 2

Selected Facts and Viewpoints

- 17 000 children under the age of five are admitted to hospital every year with illnesses resulting from passive smoking.
- The UK Government earned around £9616 million in revenue from tobacco taxes and VAT in 2003.
- Smoking kills 114 000 people every year in the UK.
- 25% of smokers said they would avoid places where the ban was in force.
- A six-month ban on smoking in public places in an American town reduced the number of heart attacks by almost 50%.
- In a survey, seven out of ten people did not support a ban on smoking in pubs, restaurants and clubs.
- It has been found that a smoke-free environment encourages smokers to reduce the number of cigarettes smoked or to quit altogether.
- In a survey, 66% agreed that the decision to allow or not to allow smoking in enclosed public places should be left up to the business owners.
- Passive smoking is thought to cause hundreds of deaths every year in the UK.

SOURCE 3

Viewpoints

The ban on smoking in enclosed public places is not only a restriction of human rights; it is also having a damaging effect on the profits of pubs and restaurants and causing job losses. Pub and restaurant owners should decide for themselves if they want to impose a ban. However, it has been found that banning smoking rarely makes financial sense. People are sick of being "nannied" by the state, with more and more laws being introduced preventing them from making choices about how they want to live their lives.

Richard Wright, restaurant owner

As a bar worker, I used to be exposed to other people's smoke throughout my working day. My clothes smelled, and I suffered many colds and sore throats. Bar work provides a valuable source of income for thousands of young people trying to help pay for their studies. It is unjust and a restriction of our human rights to risk suffering lung disease in later life. Governments have a duty to pass laws to protect workers and the public.

Reo Lazos, bar worker

You must recommend whether to continue the ban on smoking in enclosed public places (Option 1), **or** not to continue the ban on smoking in enclosed public places (Option 2), in order to improve health.

Using Sources 1, 2 and 3 above and opposite, **which option would you recommend**?

Give reasons to **support** your choice.

In your answer, you must say why you **did not recommend the other option**.

Your answer must be based on all the Sources.

(10 marks)

Reasons why you *did not recommend* the other option

After you have made your recommendation and given your reasons for choosing that option, you must say why you did not choose the other option. If you do not include this in your answer, the most you can score in this question is 8 out of 10.

You will not get marks for repeating reasons and evidence that you have already given; neither is this a summary of the points already made.

The best way to tackle this last part of the answer is to recognise a point in favour of the option you did not choose and give a counter-argument from the evidence to show why you did not choose the other option.

Consider Source 3, which gives two different views about the ban on smoking in enclosed places.

If you had chosen Option 1 – continue the ban on smoking in enclosed public places – you could write:

Reasons for not choosing Option 2

I did not choose Option 2 because, although Richard Wright, who owns a restaurant, says that the ban on smoking in enclosed public places is a restriction of human rights, Reo Lazos, who works in a bar, says that his human rights are being restricted because he will have to risk suffering lung disease later in his life. So I did not choose Option 2, because the right of people who work in bars to have a healthy life is more important than the right to smoke in enclosed public places.

If you had chosen Option 2, you could write:

Reasons for not choosing Option 1

I did not choose Option 1 because, although Reo Lazos says that bar work provides a valuable source of income for thousands of young people, Richard Wright, who owns a restaurant, says that the ban on smoking is having a damaging effect on the profits of pubs and restaurants and is causing job losses. So, if the ban continues, people like Reo Lazos may lose their jobs and not be able to earn money to support their studies.

In each of the two examples above, a point has been given which would be used to support the other option, but a counter-argument is given to show why you supported the option that you chose and did not fully accept the other argument. It shows open-mindedness and a willingness to understand another point of view but gives evidence to show why you thought the arguments for your chosen option were stronger. It is never enough to say 'I chose Option 2 because I thought the arguments were stronger' or 'I chose Option 1 because there was more evidence to support it'. Neither of these gives any evidence from the sources and would not get any marks.

Now try either of the two questions yourself. Try each question twice, first supporting Option 1 then supporting Option 2.

SELECTIVE USE OF FACTS

In this type of question, you are asked to explain why a view which is given at the end of the question is being **selective in the use of facts**. Selectivity means that some facts have been chosen (selected) from the sources which are supportive of the view while others have been left out (not selected) since they do not support the view. While there are degrees of selectivity both within the individual sources and overall, at Intermediate 2 level it is not necessary for answers to indicate how much selectivity is being shown in the statement to get full marks. Answers which do state the extent of selectivity, however, and are of a high standard will be given high marks.

Earlier in this book we used an example from football to help explain differences. Let's use another example to help explain what we mean by 'being selective in the use of facts'.

The factfile below gives information about Modern United Football Club:

Modern United Football Club Factfile
- MUFC are second bottom of the league.
- MUFC have won their last four games.
- Last year, MUFC won the Scottish Cup.
- They have won only six out of their 20 games this season.
- MUFC have had more goals scored against them than any other team in the league this season.
- This year, they were knocked out of the cup in the first round.

Modern United Football Club is an excellent football team.

View of MUFC Manager

In the very simple example above, based on one source with six pieces of information, we can see that the MUFC manager has been selective in his use of the facts. Out of the six facts in the factfile, the manager seems only to have selected the two that show MUFC doing well:

- MUFC have won their last four games
- Last year, MUFC won the Scottish Cup

... and ignored the other four parts of the factfile which show they are doing poorly

Therefore, the manager has been very selective, since out of the six points in the factfile he has based his view on only two, which support his view, and seems to have ignored the four points which do not support his view.

At Intermediate 2, you need to explain why the viewpoint is showing selectivity by giving evidence which has been ignored because it does not agree with the view and also by giving evidence that has been selected (chosen) because it agrees with the view. Since the view may be very selective or hardly selective, you do not have to have an equal amount of information that has been chosen and an equal amount of information that has been ignored.

Using the information and view above, answer the following question:

Explain why the MUFC Manager is being **selective in the use of facts**.

The Modern United Football Club Manager is being selective when he says MUFC are an excellent football team because the factfile shows that MUFC are second bottom of the league, they have only won six games out of 20 this season, they have had more goals scored against them than any other team and they were knocked out of the cup in the first round this year. These points show that MUFC are not doing well and are not an excellent team.

However, the MUFC Manager is not being selective when he says they are an excellent team because last season MUFC won the Scottish Cup and this season they have won their last four games, so he has chosen to use this evidence from the factfile to say they are an excellent team.

Up until this point in the answer, evidence has been given from the source, and there is balance in the answer because evidence has been given of information which the manager has ignored and of information which he has chosen. You could, in addition, go on to say:

The manager has been very selective in saying that MUFC is an excellent football team since he has only selected two of the six pieces of evidence in the factfile to support his view and ignored most of the statements which do not agree with his view.

It is important that the answer makes reference to the viewpoint; this should help to keep the answer to the point and show that the evidence being used is relevant. Answers which immediately give evidence from the sources but do not say if the evidence shows whether the view is being selective or not often lose marks or even get no marks at all, since it is not clear whether or not the question has actually been understood.

For full marks, you must show balance in your answer, i.e. you should show evidence that has been left out since it disagrees with the viewpoint, but you must also give examples of evidence that has been chosen since it supports the viewpoint. Balance does not have to be 50:50, and it is perfectly acceptable for most of the evidence to not support the view while one developed point makes reference to the evidence that has been selected because it supports the view.

EXAM EXAMPLE 5

Intermediate 2, 2006 paper, question 2(c)

SOURCE 1

Representation in the Scottish and UK Parliaments

The Scottish Parliament is elected by a system of proportional representation called the Additional Member System (AMS). The UK Parliament is elected using the First Past the Post (FPTP) system of election.

Under AMS, each voter has two votes, and two types of Members of the Scottish Parliament (MSPs) are elected. Each voter has a constituency MSP to represent them and also seven regional MSPs elected from party lists. In the UK Parliament, each constituency has one Member of Parliament (MP) whose role is to represent the whole constituency. Because there is a single MP representing the whole constituency, most voters would know the name of their MP.

Many believe that AMS is more representative because the result of the election is more likely to be a government made up of more than one party. Others believe FPTP is better because a single-party government is more likely to be elected and therefore to be able to put its policies into practice

In the 2003 election for the Scottish Parliament, 51 female MSPs were elected. This is almost 40% of MSPs; one of the highest figures for female representation in any parliament around the world. In the same election, there were no MSPs elected from ethnic minority communities.

After the election to the House of Commons in 2005, 128 female MPs were elected out of a total of 646, which is 20% of the total. Fifteen ethnic minority MPs were also elected.

SOURCE 2
Political Party Composition of UK and Scottish Parliaments

UK Parliament after 2005 Election	
Party	**MPs**
Labour Party	355
Conservative Party	198
Liberal Democrats	62
SNP	6
Scottish Socialist Party	0
Green Party	0
Other Parties & Independents	25
Total	**646**

- **Labour Government elected**
- **Majority of 64**

Scottish Parliament after 2003 Election	
Party	**MSPs**
Labour Party	50
Conservative Party	18
Liberal Democrats	17
SNP	27
Scottish Socialist Party	6
Green Party	7
Other Parties & Independents	4
Total	**129**

- **Labour and Liberal Democrat coalition formed**
- **Majority of 5**

Continued on next page

SOURCE 3
Survey of Public Opinion

Question:

Do you think that the Additional Member System (AMS) is better than First Past the Post (FPTP)?

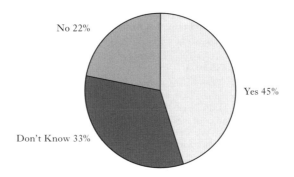

> The Additional Member System (AMS), used to elect the Scottish Parliament, is more representative and more popular with voters than the First Past the Post system.

View of Scottish Politician

Using Sources 1, 2 and 3, explain why the Scottish Politician is being **selective in the use of facts**.

Your answer must be based entirely on the Sources above and opposite.

(8 marks)

This question gives information about the results of the voting systems used to elect the Scottish and UK Parliaments and the results of a public-opinion survey about voting systems.

A point about how representative each system is in representing women and ethnic minorities could be given from Source 1 alone.

This is a good point

The Scottish Politician is being selective when he says that the Additional Member System (AMS), used to elect the Scottish Parliament, is more representative than the First Past the Post system. It is true that it is more representative of women, since in the Scottish Parliament 40% of MSPs are women and this is one of the highest figures in the world, while the House of Commons only has 20% of MPs who are female. However, if we look at ethnic minorities, he is being selective because he has not used the evidence which shows that, after the 2003 election, there were no ethnic minority MSPs elected but in the House of Commons there were 15 ethnic minority MPs elected in 2005. Therefore, the politician is being fairly selective, as what he has said is correct about women but not about ethnic minorities.

This is a good point, although it only uses evidence from one source. It compares information about women and ethnic minorities in the two parliaments; it shows balance and comes to a conclusion about how selective the view is.

High-quality answers link information between sources. Information in Source 1 about coalition governments being more likely to be formed than one-party majority governments when the Additional Member System is used could be backed up by giving information from Source 2 which shows the types of governments elected in 2003 and 2005, i.e. a majority government after the 2005 election using First Past the Post and a coalition formed in Scotland in 2003 after using the AMS system.

Use the information in Sources 1 and 2 to write an answer which links information to show selectivity in the use of facts.

Using abbreviations – There are some terms you may have to use several times in an answer. If they are long terms or phrases, this may take up quite a bit of time. Terms such as 'Additional Member System' or 'African National Congress' should be used in full the first time you refer to them, but after that you can use the abbreviations 'AMS' and 'ANC'.

Using evidence from a pie chart

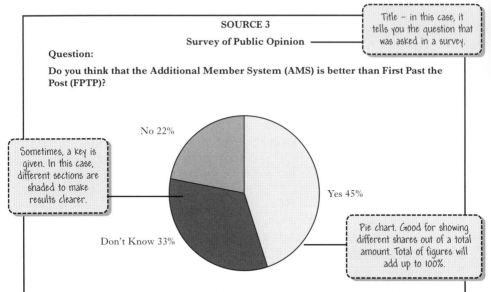

SOURCE 3

Survey of Public Opinion

Title – in this case, it tells you the question that was asked in a survey.

Question:

Do you think that the Additional Member System (AMS) is better than First Past the Post (FPTP)?

No 22%

Sometimes, a key is given. In this case, different sections are shaded to make results clearer.

Yes 45%

Don't Know 33%

Pie chart. Good for showing different shares out of a total amount. Total of figures will add up to 100%.

In this question, part of the view says 'The Additional Member System ... is ... more popular with voters than the First Past the Post system'.

By looking at the pie chart, this does seem to be the case, since the largest percentage in the survey said that they thought that the Additional Member System was better than First Past the Post, so this section of the answer could say the following:

This is a good use of statistics.

The Scottish Politician is not being selective when he says that AMS is more popular with voters than FPTP, because the results of a survey of public opinion in Source 3 show that 45% of people thought that AMS was better than FPTP while only 22% did not think it was better. Therefore the politician is right and not selective in the use of facts.

This is a perfectly valid interpretation of the results of the survey, although it would also be correct to go beyond this and include the 'Don't Knows' in your answer.

This is a better use of statistics.

The Scottish Politician is being slightly selective when he says that AMS is more popular with voters than FPTP because the results of a survey of public opinion in Source 3 show that the largest percentage of people, 45%, thought that AMS was better than FPTP compared with 22% who not think it was better. However, less than half of all people asked thought that AMS was better, because 33% did not know if AMS was better than FPTP, so more than half either did not think AMS was better or did not know.

How selective is the view?

A view may be given which is completely true and has not been selective in the use of the information at all, since all the information supports the view. On the other hand, a view might be said to be totally selective since it is not supported at all by any of the evidence in the sources. It is most likely that views given may be in between. For example, a view might be **slightly selective** if most of the information supports the view but some parts of the evidence do not support the view. The view may be **very selective** if most of the evidence contradicts the view and only a small part of the evidence is supportive. The view will be **partially selective** or **fairly selective** if the evidence seems to be fairly evenly balanced with some supporting the view and about the same amount opposing the view.

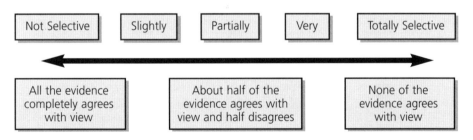

In the following question from the study theme on the United States of America, the view is given:

> **Compared to White Americans, all ethnic minorities in the USA suffer poorer health and have less access to health care.**
>
> *View of an American doctor*
>
> **Using Sources 1, 2 and 3, explain why the American doctor is being *selective in the use of facts*.**

In the answer to this question, it would be better to split the view into two parts – the section which refers to poorer health would make more use of the evidence in Sources 2 and 3, while the section on access to health care will make more reference to the evidence in Source 1.

EXAM EXAMPLE 6

Intermediate 2, 2007 paper, question 7(c)

(c)   Study Sources 1, 2 and 3 below and opposite, then answer the question which follows.

SOURCE 1

Health Insurance Factfile

Turnout has varied considerably in elections in the UK. The highest turnout for a general election in the UK was 83·9% in 1950. Since that date, election turnout has never been as high. The lowest point in general election turnout came in 2001, although it rose again in 2005. From the 1960s to the 1990s, turnout in UK general elections was always above 70%.

One factor which seems to have an effect upon turnout is how powerful and important is the parliament or council being elected. If voters see the result of the election having a big effect upon their lives, they will be more likely to vote. If the parliament or council is not seen as being so important then they will be less likely to vote. Younger voters seem to be less interested in voting than those in older age groups.

Where you live seems to have an effect upon whether or not people vote. In some parts of the country, there are many safe seats; in others there are more marginal seats. Voters are more likely to vote in those areas where the result is close so their vote may have more effect on the overall result.

The USA spends huge amounts of money on health care. The health care costs of most Americans are met by private health insurance that they pay for themselves or is provided by their employers. There are two government schemes for elderly and poor Americans – Medicare and Medicaid. Large numbers of Americans, however, have no health care insurance at all and must pay their own medical bills if they become ill. In 2003, 245 million people in the USA had health insurance coverage – 84·4% of the population. An estimated 15·6% of the population, or 45 million people, were without any health insurance coverage, an increase from 15·2% in 2002.

The percentage of Black Americans without insurance did not change. It was 20% and for Asian Americans about 19%. The percentage of whites without health insurance increased from 10·7% to 11·1%. The uninsured rate for Hispanics was 33% in 2003 – the same figure as in 2002. The actual number of Hispanics without health insurance increased from 12·8 million to 13·2 million due to population growth. The percentage of American Indian and Alaskan Native who were without medical insurance cover was 27·5%.

Of the 245 million Americans with some form of health insurance coverage in 2003, 60·4% were covered by employment-based and private schemes. The percentage of people covered by government health insurance programmes such as Medicaid and Medicare rose from 25·7% to 26·6%.

Continued on next page

SOURCE 2

Life Expectancy (in years) by Ethnic Origin and Gender

	Male	Female
Total Population	74·1	79·8
White	74·7	80·1
Black	68·4	75·1
American Indian or Alaskan Native	72·9	82·0
Asian	80·9	86·5
Hispanic	77·2	83·7

SOURCE 3

Infant Mortality Rate
Infant deaths per 1000 live births

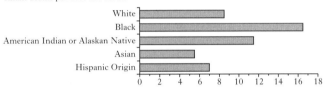

Breast Cancer Rate
Deaths per 100 000 women

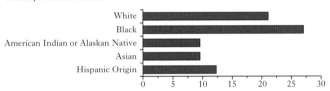

> Compared to White Americans, all ethnic minorities in the USA suffer poorer health and have less access to health care.

View of an American doctor

Using Sources 1, 2 and 3, explain why the American doctor is being **selective in the use of facts**.

Your answer must be based entirely on the Sources above and opposite.

(8 marks)

The explanation of selectivity can be included throughout the answer:

This is a good point.

The American doctor is being selective in the use of facts when she states that 'compared to White Americans, all ethnic minorities in the USA suffer poorer health': Source 2 shows us figures for life expectancy. White males have a higher figure for life expectancy, at 74·7 years, compared with the US average of 74·1 years, and it is also true that life expectancy for white males is higher than for both Blacks, who are only expected to live to 68·4 years, and American Indian or Alaskan Natives, whose life expectancy is 72·9 years. However, both Asian male life expectancy which is 80·9 years and male Hispanic life expectancy at 77·2 years are higher than White males. Therefore the American doctor is being selective, since some ethnic minorities suffer poorer health, as measured by life expectancy, compared to White Americans but not all of them.

Why is this is a good point?

In the paragraph above, the answer shows selectivity although it does not make a statement about how selective the view is. However, the last sentence could be amended slightly to include such a statement, and this could be given an additional mark:

Therefore the American doctor is being **fairly** selective since some ethnic minorities suffer poorer health, as measured by life expectancy, compared to White Americans but not all of them.

When looking at the second part of the viewpoint, the evidence to explain selectivity in the use of facts will largely come from Source 1 and start off by saying that the view is not selective:

This is a good point.

The American doctor is not being selective when she says that 'compared to White Americans, all ethnic minorities in the USA have less access to health care' since Source 1 shows us that, of all the ethnic groups mentioned, Whites do have the lowest percentage of people without health insurance. Only 11·1% of Whites are without health insurance, while for Black Americans it is 20%, for Asian Americans it is 19% without health insurance, 33% of Hispanics do not have health insurance and 27·5% of American Indians do not have health insurance. Therefore, when she says all ethnic minorities have less access to health care, she is not being selective in the use of evidence.

CONCLUSIONS

In this type of question, you have to come to a judgement based upon the evidence given in the sources. Some candidates write out large amounts of information in this type of question but only repeat or paraphrase the evidence given without actually coming to any conclusions about the significance or meaning of the evidence.

Conclusions can be varied and may refer to well-thought-out and evidence-based judgements such as:

- The extent to which something has changed or remained the same
- Biggest, smallest etc.
- Trends over time
- Comparisons between different groups
- How successful ...
- How effective ...

Since a large amount of information is given in the sources, and since many and varied conclusions can be drawn, it is essential that you use the bullet-pointed prompts in the questions to organise your answers. You must attempt to draw conclusions about **at least three** of the given prompts.

It is good practice to use the prompts as headings before using the evidence to draw conclusions. The conclusions do not need to appear at the end of the evidence, although this is a perfectly acceptable approach.

Using Sources 1, 2 and 3 above and opposite, what **conclusions** can be drawn about turnout in elections in Britain?

You should reach conclusions about at least **three** of the following:

- changes over time
- age of voters
- the parliament or council being elected
- area of the UK.

You must use information from all the Sources. You should compare information within and between the Sources.

(8 marks)

You will be able to score full marks by giving conclusions about three of the bullet points. Don't just do the first three. Look at all the bullet points and decide which three you wish to include in your answer.

EXAM EXAMPLE 7

Intermediate 2, 2007 paper, question 2(d)

Question 2 (continued)

(*d*) Study Sources 1, 2 and 3 below and opposite, then answer the question which follows.

SOURCE 1

2005 General Election: percentage (%) turnout by age group and area

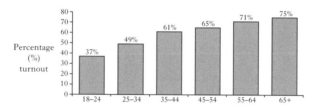

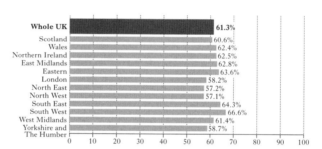

SOURCE 2

Turnout in Parliament and Council Elections

Election	Year	Turnout %
UK General Election	2005	61·5%
UK General Election	2001	59·4%
Scottish Parliament Election	2003	49·4%
Scottish Parliament Election	1999	59·1%
European Parliament Election	2004	38·4%
European Parliament Election	1999	24·0%
English Local Council Elections	2004	40·1%
Scottish Local Council Elections	2003	49·2%
Welsh Local Council Elections	2004	43·2%
Northern Ireland Local Council Elections	2001	66·0%

Continued on next page

Question 2 (d) (continued)

SOURCE 3

Election Turnout in the United Kingdom

Turnout has varied considerably in elections in the UK. The highest turnout for a general election in the UK was 83·9% in 1950. Since that date, election turnout has never been as high. The lowest point in general election turnout came in 2001, although it rose again in 2005. From the 1960s to the 1990s, turnout in UK general elections was always above 70%.

One factor which seems to have an effect upon turnout is how powerful and important is the parliament or council being elected. If voters see the result of the election having a big effect upon their lives, they will be more likely to vote. If the parliament or council is not seen as being so important, then they will be less likely to vote. Younger voters seem to be less interested in voting than those in older age groups.

Where you live seems to have an effect upon whether or not people vote. In some parts of the country, there are many safe seats; in others there are more marginal seats. Voters are more likely to vote in those areas where the result is close, so their vote may have more effect on the overall result.

Using Sources 1, 2 and 3 above and opposite, what **conclusions** can be drawn about turnout in elections in Britain?

You should reach conclusions about at least **three** of the following:

• changes over time

• age of voters

• the parliament or council being elected

• area of the UK.

You must use information from all the Sources. You should compare information within and between the Sources.

(8 marks)

In the first example, the evidence relating to 'Turnout and the Parliament or Council being elected' is given first, and the conclusion is reached towards the end of the paragraph.

Evidence first

then

conclusion reached at end

Turnout and the Parliament or Council being elected

Source 2 shows me that turnout for the UK Parliament General Election was 61·5% in 2005, for the Scottish Parliament in 2003 it was 49·4% and for the European Parliament it in 2004 was only 38·4%. The turnout in local council elections in England, Scotland and Wales was between 40·1% and 49·2%. Source 3 says that how powerful and important the parliament or council is will affect turnout. My conclusion is that turnout is different for different parliaments and councils, and the UK Parliament has the highest turnout while the European Parliament has the lowest turnout because voters think the UK Parliament is the most important and powerful while the European Parliament is less important.

Alternatively, you may reach a conclusion at the beginning of the section and then go on to use the evidence, drawn from two sources, to provide support for the conclusion reached:

Conclusion at start

Evidence proves conclusion

Turnout and the Age of Voters

My conclusion is that older age groups are more likely to vote than younger age groups. The evidence for this conclusion is shown in Source 1, where only 37% of the 18-24 age group voted in the 2005 General Election while 65% of the age group 45-54 voted and the highest figure of 75% turnout was for the 65+ age group. In Source 3, it also says that 'younger voters seem to be less interested in voting than those in older age groups'.

In the question which follows, you are asked to draw conclusions from the sources given about elections in South Africa. Sources 1 and 2 contain a large amount of statistical information in the form of tables, and Source 3 is a written source. When you are given such a large amount of information, it is essential that you use the bullet-point prompts at the end of the question and use them to organise your answer. You must choose at least three of these, about which you will draw conclusions.

Conclusions are not just rewriting the information in the sources – you must study the evidence and reach a judgement about the information. Not all of the information is equally important. Some information in the sources is more important than other information, and it is the important or significant information you should focus on in your answer.

EXAM EXAMPLE 8

Intermediate 2, 2006 paper, question 9(d)

(*d*) Study Sources 1, 2 and 3 below and opposite, then answer the question which follows.

SOURCE 1

National Assembly Election Results, 1999 and 2004

Party	1999		2004	
	Votes (%)	Seats	Votes (%)	Seats
African National Congress (ANC)	66·3%	266	69·6%	279
Democratic Alliance (DA)	9·5%	38	12·3%	50
New National Party (NNP)	6·9%	28	1·7%	7
Inkatha Freedom Party (IFP)	6·6%	34	6·9%	28
United Democratic Movement (UDM)	3·4%	14	2·3%	9
African Christian Democratic Party (ACDP)	1·4%	6	1·6%	6
Freedom Front (FF)	0·8%	3	0·9%	4
Pan Africanist Congress (PAC)	0·7%	3	0·7%	3
Others	4·4%	8	4·0%	14
Total	100%	400	100%	400
Number of registered voters	18 172 751		20 674 926	
Voter turnout	89·3%		76·7%	

SOURCE 2

Provincial Seats Won, 2004

Region \ Party	ANC	DA	NNP	IFP	UDM	ACDP	FF	PAC	Others
Eastern Cape	51	5	0	0	6	0	0	1	0
Free State	25	3	0	0	0	1	1	0	0
Gauteng	51	15	0	2	1	1	1	1	1
KwaZulu Natal	38	7	0	30	1	2	0	0	2
Mpumalanga	27	2	0	0	0	0	1	0	0
Northern Cape	21	3	2	0	0	1	1	0	2
Limpopo	45	2	0	0	1	1	0	0	0
North West	27	2	0	0	0	0	1	0	3
Western Cape	19	12	5	0	1	2	0	0	3

A report compiled by the Election Observer Mission (EOM) said that the elections were, on the whole, conducted in a peaceful, orderly and open manner.

Continued on next page

SOURCE 3

South African Elections

In South Africa, the ANC celebrated another victory in the 2004 general election, which was declared free and fair. The ANC won the majority of seats in the National Assembly, obtaining its first-ever two-thirds majority. It also did very well in the provincial elections, winning KwaZulu Natal and Western Cape for the first time. The ANC's majority has also increased at national level. The Election Observer Mission (EOM) concluded that the elections were a true reflection of the will of the people of South Africa. President Thabo Mbeki also congratulated all political parties who contested the election and thanked them for readily accepting the final results 'even in those instances in which the outcome was not as favourable as they might have expected'. The President expressed relief at the fact that political tensions in KwaZulu Natal did not spoil the election. The EOM did note that the conduct of the elections in a few areas had some problems, mostly involving inconsistent voting and counting procedures. For example, some voting stations used one ballot box for both national and provincial ballot papers while others used a ballot box each for the two different papers.

A high voter turnout contradicted the predictions of voter apathy. People queued in their millions to vote in the country's third general election since the fall of apartheid. The electoral commission reported a strong turnout at most of the country's 17 000 polling stations. In some areas, people had queued from 3 am. The Western Cape and KwaZulu Natal recorded the two lowest provincial turnouts where it had been expected to be higher due to the contest between the ANC and the opposition parties.

Using Sources 1, 2 and 3, what **conclusions** can be reached about the elections in South Africa?

You should reach conclusions about at least **three** of the following:

- support for political parties at national level
- support for political parties at provincial level
- voter turnout and registration
- the conduct of the elections.

You must use information from all of the Sources above and opposite. You should compare information within and between the Sources.

(8 marks)

The first thing to do when answering a question of this type is to find out what the sources are about. You do not need to read each source in detail in order to do this. A quick scan will give you a rough idea of the information contained in each source. For the tables, the main parts to look at first are the headings and subheadings. At this stage, you will not pay any real attention to the detailed information in the columns of figures.

In written sources, just like in statistical sources, the first thing to do is read the title. If the source contains several paragraphs, reading the first sentence in each will give you a broad idea of what the source contains – you are not looking for the detailed information in the source yet.

Scanning the source

1 Title – tells you the table has election results for the National Assembly for two elections 1999 and 2004

2 Column headings – gives more detail than in the title. Information for each election in votes (%) and seats

SOURCE 1

National Assembly Election Results, 1999 and 2004

2 Column heading – lists the parties in the election

Party	1999		2004	
	Votes (%)	Seats	Votes (%)	Seats
African National Congress (ANC)	66·3%	266	69·6%	279
Democratic Alliance (DA)	9·5%	38	12·3%	50
New National Party (NNP)	6·9%	28	1·7%	7
Inkatha Freedom Party (IFP)	6·6%	34	6·9%	28
United Democratic Movement (UDM)	3·4%	14	2·3%	9
African Christian Democratic Party (ACDP)	1·4%	6	1·6%	6
Freedom Front (FF)	0·8%	3	0·9%	4
Pan Africanist Congress (PAC)	0·7%	3	0·7%	3
Others	4·4%	8	4·0%	14
Total	**100%**	**400**	**100%**	**400**
Number of registered voters	**18 172 751**		**20 674 926**	
Voter turnout	**89·3%**		**76·7%**	

3 At the bottom of the table (in bold), additional information gives total figures and information about number of registered voters and turnout

4 Detailed information which you will use in your answer but you do not need to study in much detail when scanning

By quickly scanning the source, without spending time at this stage in looking at the detailed information in the table, you will already have a fairly good idea about the evidence that the source contains.

You should do the same for the other sources in the question before you look at the bullet points.

By looking at Source 2 (page 105), the title tells you that this gives information about 'Provincial seats won, 2004'. The parties are shown along the top of each column, and the Regions of South Africa are shown in the first column of the table. There is some additional information given at the bottom of the table which should not be ignored. You should not assume that the important information is all at the beginning of the table – important information is just as likely to be at the end of the table.

Source 3 (page 106) is written. The heading only tells you it is about South African elections, so you can assume it is a fairly general source of information – but even reading the first sentences in each paragraph gives you some idea of what it contains.

Now that you have familiarised yourself with the sort of information contained in the sources, you need to look at what you should draw conclusions about. You are given four bullet points. You do not have to do all four. If you do attempt all four, you may end up spending too much time on the question or only drawing simple and basic conclusions which do not make much use of the evidence.

> Using Sources 1, 2 and 3, what **conclusions** can be reached about the elections in South Africa?
>
> You should reach conclusions about at least **three** of the following:
>
> * support for political parties at national level
> * support for political parties at provincial level
> * voter turnout and registration
> * the conduct of the elections.
>
> You must use information from all of the Sources above and opposite. You should compare information within and between the Sources.
>
> **(8 marks)**

The first bullet point you are asked to reach a conclusion about is:

● support for political parties at national level.

From your first scan of the sources, you already know that Source 1 contains information about the National Assembly election result, so you will be using evidence from this source. Source 2 is about the results in the Provinces – so this is unlikely to contain information for this conclusion. In Source 3, even by only having read the first sentence, you will have seen that this tells you that 'the ANC celebrated another victory in the 2004 general election …', so you will find information in this source to help you reach conclusions for this first bullet point.

You should use the bullet point as a heading in your answer:

Support for political parties at national level

Your Modern Studies experience and skills will probably tell you, before you look at the evidence, that the most important and significant conclusions are likely to be about such things as 'the biggest party', 'the party which won the election', the size of its majority over other parties', 'the parties that are growing in strength or the parties that are declining in strength'.

 It can be very helpful to use a highlighter when answering questions that contain a large amount of information in order to pick out the significant information you are going to use in your conclusions.

SOURCE 3

South African Elections

In South Africa, the ANC celebrated another victory in the 2004 general election, which was declared free and fair. The ANC won the majority of seats in the National Assembly, obtaining its first-ever two-thirds majority. It also did very well in the provincial elections, winning KwaZulu Natal and Western Cape for the first time. The ANC's majority has also increased at national level. The Election Observer Mission (EOM) concluded that the elections were a true reflection of the will of the people of South Africa. President Thabo Mbeki also congratulated all political parties who contested the election and thanked them for readily accepting the final results 'even in

The parts of Source 3 which are highlighted above refer to the result of the national election and refer to the main party, the ANC. This information and any other points which refer to the topic of the first conclusion can be linked with the evidence in Source 1 to draw relevant and valid conclusions.

Support for political parties at national level

Although Source 1 shows that South Africa has many different political parties at the national level [1], the African National Congress is the largest and most successful party [2]. Source 3 states that the ANC celebrated another victory in the 2004 general election and that they increased their majority at a national level [3]. Source 1 backs this up by showing that in 1999 they won 266 seats and in 2004 this increased to 279 seats [4]. Compared with the other parties at national level, the ANC is by far the largest since it has 279 out of 400 seats in the National Assembly, while the second biggest party, the Democratic Alliance, only has 50 seats and the third party, the Inkatha Freedom Party, has only 28 [4].

[1] Basic conclusion without any evidence being given in support.

[2] Another conclusion about the ANC being the largest party, supported by evidence from:

[3] Source 3 evidence

[4] Source 1 evidence which, when combined with the evidence from Source 3, backs up the conclusion [2] made.

For each of the questions in this section, draw conclusions about each of the points where answers have not already been given.

Conclusion

Now that you have worked through the different sections in this book, We hope you feel much more confident about tackling your Intermediate Modern Studies exam.

No single book can give you everything you need to do well, but the advice contained in the various chapters of this book should help you to make better use of the information you have gained in class, by watching news programmes on television, reading newspapers and using the Internet.

The information in Chapters 1 and 2 will help you to write better answers to Knowledge and Understanding questions. To do well in this type of question, you must also study hard in class. Listen to what your teacher or lecturer tells you. Do regular revision, using your notes and textbooks. Keep up to date with what is going on in the topics you are studying in school by watching the news on TV, reading a newspaper regularly and surfing the Net. There will always be new information about the topics you have studied – this will improve your knowledge and understanding and give you examples that you can include in your answers to impress the examiners.

Chapters 3 and 4 will help you develop skills that will improve your examination performance. These skills are also useful throughout your life to help you make sense of what is going on in the world today and in the future. Making decisions, drawing conclusions, detecting exaggeration and selective use of facts are skills that you will call upon repeatedly and make you a better and more informed citizen. Skills need to be practised regularly. You should practise exam questions from past papers in order to improve your skills. You can also practise these skills at other times. If you read a newspaper article, think if the information is being presented in an exaggerated way. What conclusions can you draw about an opinion poll reported on the news? What decision would you make about an issue your friends are talking about?

Modern Studies is a great subject. It is always changing, so it is always interesting. The topics in Modern Studies affect the way you live your life and give you an insight into the lives of people in other societies. The information in this book will help you to do well in your Modern Studies course and gain a good qualification. You will also become a better citizen able to make informed decisions and play a fuller part in the society in which you live.